Boutique Thinking in a Big Box World

Boutique Thinking in a Big Box World

◆

A Caffeinated Instruction Manual for Open Minded Sales Enthusiasts

Joe Marcoux

iUniverse, Inc.
New York Lincoln Shanghai

Boutique Thinking in a Big Box World
A Caffeinated Instruction Manual for Open Minded Sales Enthusiasts

Copyright © 2007 by Joel Marcoux

iUniverse books may be ordered through booksellers or by contacting:

iUniverse
2021 Pine Lake Road, Suite 100
Lincoln, NE 68512
www.iuniverse.com
1-800-Authors (1-800-288-4677)

Because of the dynamic nature of the Internet, any Web addresses or links contained in this book may have changed since publication and may no longer be valid.

The views expressed in this work are solely those of the author and do not necessarily reflect the views of the publisher, and the publisher hereby disclaims any responsibility for them.

ISBN: 978-0-595-44527-1 (pbk)
ISBN: 978-0-595-68828-9 (cloth)
ISBN: 978-0-595-88855-9 (ebk)

Printed in the United States of America

To my incredible daughters, Simone and Katrine. To my best friend and love, Tammy.
Finally, to my various mentors whom I continue to learn from.
From my heart, thank you.

Contents

Introduction

The story you are about to read unfolds like a movie script.
If there is one thing I've learned, it is in dialogue and in relationship that we can truly acquire knowledge. So, it seemed right to have this story play out as if you could picture it on the big screen.

The following story should be served in small amounts, like a good cup of coffee. I encourage you to savor and enjoy it.
A good coffee should be shared, and so should this book.

As the story unfolds, there will be areas where you are invited to write in your own answers or discoveries. Have members of your team do the same. Share your ideas and continue to be inspired!

The Daily Grind

Handing the couple a brochure and his business card, Martin said "Goodbye" to his 3rd set of customers in 2 hours. Traffic at the store had been relative to the same time last year; unfortunately the results in the till were much slimmer.

Martin was in a slump, and if the "pep talk" from his boss, Mr. Hobbs were any indication, things had to get better or he was going to be building on his résumé. The young man, originally passionate about the opportunity to work in an industry that held his attention and interest, set the alarm and locked the door for the night.

Martin met Jen, his fiancée, for dinner at "their" local restaurant. This was their time to unwind.

Jen: "Hey sweetie. How was your day?"

Martin: "Hi Jen. Let's start with you today OK?"

Jen paused, smiled and cried out: "I aced my exam!"

Martin: "Aw Jen that's great. You really made it happen girl. I'm happy for you."

Another pause from Jen: "OK, what's wrong?"

Martin: "C'mon Jen. Let's make tonight about you."

Jen: "Let's not. It's about us"

The appetizers arrived at the table.
Jen: "So what gives?"

Martin: "My sales suck, Jen. I'm dying inside. I'm afraid of losing my job and the more I think about it, the more I mess up at work. It's a vicious cycle."

Jen listened to her future husband spill the beans on the "pep talk" that Mr. Hobbs gave him. Martin was venting once again about lack of advertising, the location of the store and how these big box stores have them surrounded and are squeezing the life out of them.

Jen: "Can I offer you some feedback?"

Martin: "Here we go."

Jen: "Come on Martin. Really. If you don't want my feedback just say 'No'."

Martin: "OK. I'm listening."

Jen: "Have you thought of picking up a sales book or something? I mean, it's a start right?"

Martin: "I've read that stuff before. It's all the same. I feel weird using "techniques" that suggest lying to customers."

Jen: "Come on. It's not that bad. Why don't you go to the bookstore before work tomorrow, browse and get yourself a coffee while you're at it? Keep an open mind. What have you got to lose?"

"Keep an open mind."

Martin: "At this point. Not much I guess. At least I can get a good cup of coffee before work."

Martin regularly complained to his fiancée that the location of the store wasn't particularly great, and that the owner was cheap because he wasn't advertising enough, and because of that there weren't enough quality customers walking through the door. In the same breath, Martin would then complain that he needed better help with his staff when things did get busy in the store. For Martin things got busy when more than 2 customers were in at the same time.

For the 2 years that Martin has worked in Mr. Hobbs' store, a couple of products have had national ad campaigns and solid media exposure. In hindsight, Martin's previous sales success was the result of simply being an "order taker".

Time For Coffee

Feeling really good about making the decision to improve his game, Martin entered the coffee shop area of the bookstore, before browsing the various selections. With his double shot latté in hand, Martin began his mission.

He headed to the business section and was shocked to see the volumes of books on selling, career management, time management, quality, and a section called "six sigma"?

Martin must have had quite the look on his face because a man down the isle said to him: "You OK? Looks like you might need another one of those!"

The man was casually dressed and had one of those genuine smiles, like a good neighbor you actually want to sit down and have coffee with.

Martin: "Uh, Yeah. I'm good. I'm just looking."

"Hey I didn't ask if you wanted that baby in beige or light beige did I?" said the man using a sarcastic tone.

Martin smirked: "No! Not at all! Do you work here?"

"No. I am a regular though. Nicholas Robinson." He put out his hand and Martin automatically responded in kind.

Martin: "Martin Sparks! Are you the same Nicholas Robinson who owns the NR's restaurants?"

Nic: "The same."

NR's were a popular place for a variety of reasons. The food was great and very reasonably priced. The staff was fun, helpful and attentive.

Nicholas Robinson started his first restaurant business 20 years earlier at the age of 22, which he had since sold. His recent venture had 6 new NR's locations under his belt, and they were always busy. Everyone in town knew that Nicholas Robinson had the recipe for success.

Martin: "Cool! Jen & I were at your south end location last night. Nice to meet you Mr. Robinson!"

Nic: "Call me Nic. Anyone who's a fellow study of this subject matter can dispose of the Mr. Robinson stuff. By the way, who's Jen?"

Martin: "Oh. She's my girlfriend. I mean my *fiancée*".
Martin used the similar sarcastic tone used earlier by Nic.

"Nice! You're quick Martin. I like that. Have any recommendations for me?" said Nic while waving his arm out to the huge array of books to choose from.

Martin: "Hmmm. I really don't think I'm the right guy to ask Mr. Robinson."

"Nic"

Martin: "OK … Nic. It was Jen's idea that I come here. To get me out of my slump."

Nic: "What slump is that?"

Martin: "I don't want to bother you with that."

Nic: "No-no. No bother at all. Please, what slump?"

Martin went into his telling of the story with Nic like he did the night before with Jen. Nic simply listened.

Martin: "… So that's my story and I've come here for help."

When Martin was done Nic paused for a few moments before saying: "What time do you have to be at work?"

Martin: "In a half hour."

Nic: "OK. Can I suggest a book for you?"

Martin: "Sure!"

Nic walked over to the shelf and plucked out a small book that stated it was a "best seller" and handed it to Martin.

Nic: "Start with this" I recommend it to all my new staff.

The book was called Who Moved My Cheese by Spencer Johnson.

Martin was overjoyed!

1.   He just got free advice from a local business hero.

2.   The book was small and would take no time to read at all.

Martin: "Thanks Nic!"

Nic: "My pleasure. I'm always happy to give a hand."

As he was at the till paying for the book, Martin saw Nic go to the coffee counter.
Martin said to the cashier: "I'll pay for his coffee too".
Nic smiled and said: "Thanks Martin. That's really not necessary. Just let me know what you think of the book".

Martin: "I insist. And I sure will".

Always Be Open To Ask

Martin would be the first to say, he's not fond of reading: "Jen, I can fall asleep reading the sports page!"

Jen persisted: "C'mon Martin. You even said it's a small book. And if Nicholas Robinson recommended it, it's a great start. One page at a time OK?"

Martin: "One page at a time."

It took 5 persistent days for Martin to finish the book and on the 6th day, he headed for the coffee shop at the bookstore to get a well-deserved Java before work.

"This one's on me." said Nic catching Martin by surprise.

Martin: "Hey! Thanks! Do you live here or what?"

Nic: "Ha! Yeah. I sleep in the home improvement section. Like I told you, I'm a regular. Got time to sit?"

Martin: "Sure!"

They sat at a corner table in large comfortable chairs with their frothy jet fuelled lattés.

Nic: "So what'd you think of the first book?"

Martin didn't like the sound of "first book".

"It was good." said Martin.

Nic smiled.

"What's so funny?" asked Martin.

"What did you learn?" said Nic.

Martin paused: "I learned the importance of accepting change and based on the fact that you said "first book" earlier, I figure I better learn to enjoy reading more."

Nic laughed: "Nice!"

Martin: "Thanks."

Nic: "How's the slump?"

Martin: "Still slumping for the moment."

Nic: "Hmmm. That will change. You'll see." Nic paused: "Can I ask you a question?"

Martin: "Sure."

Nic: "What do you do in life?"

Martin: "I thought I already told you."

Nic: "No, you told me where you work. You told me what products you sell. You didn't tell me what you do in life."

Martin didn't know how to answer the question and Nic could tell. "How 'bout you chew on that question for a while? When you reflect you will attract the answer."

Martin: "Reflect?"
Nic: "Yeah. Reflect as in embody it. When you do that, the answers will come."

"When you reflect, you will attract."

Nic: "When you reflect you think deeply and carefully about what you want and do. And at the same time you're bouncing that thought away from you. So keep thinking about it."

Martin: "I think I'm going to have to."

They sipped their coffees and Martin asked: "How'd you make it Nic?"

Nic: "Whoa! Loaded question there Martin"

Martin: "Sorry. I don't mean to pry."

Nic: "You're not prying Martin. In fact, you're asking the right questions." He took a long sip of his coffee. "I always think like a Boutique storeowner. I also urge my employees to do the same."

Martin: "A boutique? But isn't a boutique small? You have several locations. You're business certainly isn't small."

Nic: "My business is growing and for that I am grateful. For me Boutique Thinking means: The way to compete against the Big Box guys."

Martin: "I'm still lost."

Nic: "Let me put it to you this way. A Boutique services a sophisticated and specialized clientele. People are getting smarter and wiser wouldn't you agree?"

Martin: "I'd say so."

Nic: "Well let's take you for example. What brought you to this bookstore in the first place?"

Martin: "It was Jen who recommended it. I figured I'd get a good cup of coffee while I was at it. I mean, how was I to know where to look?"

Nic paused, then said: "I think you did know Martin. And you have Jen to thank for the inspiration. You've come here and taken the first step. Call it "listening to your gut". And now you're getting what you asked for."

"Listen to your gut."

Nic: "A Boutique embodies the "entrepreneurial spirit" that we keep hearing about. That word "Spirit" goes hand in hand with "inspired". When you're inspired, time has no meaning, your focus is like a laser, and it would seem that dormant forces come alive to keep you in the zone."

Martin: "Wow! That's a mouthful."

Nic: "It is! Now it's time to take the next step."

Martin hesitated: "You want to help me?"

Nic: "That's what you said less than a week ago."

At that moment an older distinguished looking gentleman came by their corner and said hello to Nic.

Nic: "Martin, this is Richard Caan".

Martin: "I know who he is. I mean, I know who you are sir. Nice to meet you."

"Hello Martin", said Mr. Caan who stuck out his hand just like Nic did when Martin first met him. Richard Caan was the former mayor of the city. He had several different businesses and land developments all over the country.

Nic: "I meet with Richard from time to time to get some advice. He's one of my mentors. In fact, if it weren't for this man, I probably wouldn't be where I am today."

Mr. Caan smiled his postcard smile and said to Nic: "Hey kid, I get a lot of juice from our meetings too."

Martin was reeling. Maybe it was the nuclear coffee or simply the moment. Either way, Martin looked at Nic and said: "Nic, can you be a mentor to me?"

Nic: "Martin, I'm proud of you already. Truth is, I volunteered 6 days ago"

Mr. Caan chuckled & Nic smiled at him: "Sound familiar?"

"Spooky" said Mr. Caan. "I'm going to get a decaf. Nic, need a refill?"

Nic: "I'm good. I'll have a seat with you by the time you have your java." He then turned to Martin.

"Here's another book for you Martin", said Nic who seemingly manifested a slightly bigger book out of thin air. This book was called Bringing Out the Best in Others. It had been in his hands since Martin arrived. "Here's my card. I have another meeting here next week at 9:00 in the morning. Can you be here for 8:00?"
Martin: "You bet!"

Over the next few days Martin pushed himself to read. The material was good and the fact that he now had a real mentor like Nic in his corner, Martin felt energized like when he first started his current job as store manager. Now he needed some hands on stuff. He finished the book faster than he thought he would. He sacrificed a couple favorite TV shows and it was worth it, just for the sense of accomplishment alone. He couldn't wait to meet with his mentor!
He met with Nic at 8:00AM the following week.

"The <u>feeling</u> of accomplishment <u>inspires</u> us to do more!"

Return of The First Question

As they sat down with their respective coffees, Nic got down to business.

Nic: "How was the read?"

Martin: "I actually liked it better than the first book."

Nic: "Good. Put any thought into my question last week?"

Martin: "The one about "What I do?" Yeah, but I'd like to ask you the same question to see where you're going with this before I answer."

Nic laughed: "Nice work! OK. When it comes to NR's Restaurants, I provide people wonderful dinning experiences that are packed with value."

"Wow!" was all Martin could say. Nic was right. Everything he said was bang on. Now, Martin's wheels were turning and Nic could see it.

"This is your first major lesson Martin," said Nic. "Define who you are and what you do, and you will be headed on the highway to success. This is your mantra."

Martin: "My what?"

Nic: "Your Mantra. It's your personal slogan or statement and you should review often."

Martin never looked at his work from this kind of perspective before. He always looked at it from the angle of selling product and getting a paycheck. It's obviously more than that.

Nic: "Take the time to think about it again. Let it sit in your mind while you read your next book."

Nic handed Martin, The Trendmaster's Guide by Robyn Waters.

Nic: "Get real about what it is you are doing for your contributions at work and at home. How you define yourself affects your life."

"How you define yourself affects your life."

What I DO (My Mantra)

Take this opportunity to define what you are doing in your work. Be clear with what motivates you to do the work you do.

_____
_____
_____
_____
_____
_____
_____
_____
_____
_____

"Make your Mantra and review it Often."

Stay Focused On The Benefits

Martin was sipping on a double espresso when Nic sat down next to him.

Nic: "How's your slump?"

Martin: "Well, I can't get much worse."

Nic: "What was that?" he said laughing "positive-negativity?"

Martin with a nervous chuckle: "I guess it was."

Nic could tell that Martin was anxious about his slump.

Nic: "OK Martin, here's your next book."

This book was the biggest yet. It looked like a college textbook, Re-Imagine by Tom Peters.

Martin looked stunned: "How long will this take me to read?"

Nic: "As long as you want it to. You're choosing to do the work to improve. I'm also giving you an assignment."

Martin: "An assignment?" Now Martin was feeling like he was back at school.

Nic: "Don't be discouraged my friend. This is a flight of stairs."

Martin: "A flight of stairs eh?"

Nic: "Yeah. See yourself at the top. You may not be able to see the whole staircase right now, and that's OK. You don't need to. All you need to worry about is each step to your final destination."

Martin: "Cool. I like that."

Nic: "If you get concerned with the length of the trip, you miss the journey and probably don't reach the destination you wanted. Focus on the result you want AND on each step in the moment, the flight of stairs will take care of itself."

Martin, feeling better: "OK. So what's the next step?"

Nic: "It is a question of great importance Martin."

Martin: "OK. Shoot."

Nic: "Who Is your customer!"

Martin paused for about 1 second then said: "That's easy. Everybody!"

Nic: "Hold on there Martin. Take a closer look OK? In the last 2 years that you've been working at Mr.Hobbs' store, what would be a detailed definition of who your customer is? You can call them your "target audience" if you want."

Martin: "Hmmm. I'm going to have to 'reflect' on this one."

Nic: "Excellent. Do that. Let it sit in your gut for a while."

Martin: "Think with my gut?"

Nic: "Yeah. Most times when we know the answer, we feel it."

Martin paused, then smirked and said: "Yeah, I know that feeling."

Nic: "Sure you do. We all do!"

Nic took another sip of coffee: "I may have something to help you reflect. Have you ever heard of the 80/20 rule?"

Martin: "I think so."

Nic: "In many businesses, the 80/20 rule "generally" works like this: 80 % of your sales come from 20% of your inventory."

"Generally: 80% of your sales come from 20% of your inventory."

Nic: "I know that there are certain "signature items" on my menu that are hot sellers."

Martin: "Like your Chillied Chocolate Chicken!"

Nick: "Exactly! That's why I stock a lot of that item in the fridge of every location."

Martin: "I also see how you've marketed it to me. You have that *NR* logo next to it."

Nic: "Next to that & the other items that represent the majority of my sales."

Martin: "That's very smart."

Nic smiling: "Thank you. We track the popular items closely and test new items by making specials. If the specials get excellent feedback, they make our new menu."

Martin: "Cool stuff."

Nic: "Very. It also makes it easier for me to do inventory. So based upon the 80/20 rule, it stands to reason 80% of your sales will come from a specific market segment. We need to correctly identify & define who our customers are. And we have to continually ask ourselves who our customer is. Do you understand why?"

Martin knew the answer based on his new book:
-"Because business is changing so fast that we need to re-imagine ourselves and therefore who our customers are to stay on top of our game. End quote", said Martin with the same playful sarcasm that made Nic laugh.

Nic: "You got it! Now you can choose to take it to another level."

Martin: "How so?"

Nic: "Instead of calling your target audience a client or customer, you can choose to think of them as benefactors."

Martin: "Wow! Now that is being of service!"

Who Am I Serving?

Fill out the following details of your target benefactor.

Here are some questions to help you get a better focus on who the target benefactor is:

What is the average age of your target?

Is your target married?

Do they have Children?

Are your benefactors children?

How old are the kids?

How did they hear about your business?

Level of health (1-10 scale. 1 being low 10 being high)

Do your targets come alone, as couples or families?

Who makes the buying decision?

Who makes the payment?

Do they use financing?

Are they technology savvy? (Do they surf the Internet? Can they program their DVD player or is it flashing 12:00? Do they still use a VCR?)

What would be the average household income?

Have they ever purchased the product or service you provide before?

What is their goal?

Is the customer definition going to be the same in 5 years?

Is the benefactor comfortable in the place of business?

In what ways can that be improved?

Is the problem that they are looking to solve, possibly embarrassing? In what manner can I ask questions so my benefactor is put at ease?

Review your list of questions of who your benefactors are every 3 months. As time moves forward, the odds are that your clients will grow and change and therefore so should you!

Let's Do Lunch

When Martin heard Nic's voice at the other end of the line, he was surprised. Nic got down to business.

Nic: "Ever hear of the book Never Eat Alone by Keith Ferrazzi?"

Martin: "I'm guessing I have to put that on my education list."

Nic: "You bet. You like sushi?"

Martin: "Never tried it. I guess I never saw it on your menu."

Nic: "We don't serve it."

Martin: "Ah. Not your target audience."

Nic: "Exactly!" Nic paused, "Want to try some? My treat."

Martin: "I don't know. The thought of it kind of freaks me out. Raw fish?"

Nic laughing: "C'mon grasshopper."

The arrangements were made for their first lunch meeting.
Once they arrived at the restaurant, Nic got down to business.

Nic: "Ever hear of the word Kaizen?"

Martin: "Nope."

Nic: "It's Japanese. It means continual never ending improvement."

Martin just listened as the sushi arrived at the table. He was nervous of trying the food and not liking it.

Nic: "In business and in your personal life, think about becoming consistently better. You're doing it now Martin. You are pushing your boundaries just by trying sushi for the first time. Now you may not like the sushi, and that's OK. What does matter is you are learning, growing and pushing your limits."

Martin: "I think I get it."

Nic: "I know you do. What is pushing your limits today will be easy in the future."

"What is pushing your limits today will be easy in the future."

Martin: "What is this?" he said pointing at a piece of sushi.

Nic: "That is salmon. It will melt in your mouth. Here's the deal with this food. You have to eat the whole piece in one bite."

Martin took a deep breath and thought "OK, Kaizen". To his surprise, it tasted fantastic.

The meal was excellent, as was the conversation.

As Nic paid he looked at Martin and said, "I learned a lot today."

Martin was puzzled. "What did you learn today? I thought I was the student here."

Nic: "I came to this restaurant because I heard they were very good. I watched their systems, their service and presentation. I paid attention to your expression and level of satisfaction. In this manner I can compare with my business and apply the Kaizen method. These people are successful. I want to continue to be successful. I surround myself with the conditions I want to produce."

It was like a switch turned on for Martin: "Aw Dude, you're good."

"Surround yourself with the conditions you want to produce."

Nic laughed and gifted Martin with a book called Raving Fans by Ken Blanchard and Sheldon Bowles.

Martin: "What do I owe you for this?"

Nic: "Not a thing my friend. Just keep growing like you are."

Over the next couple of weeks, Martin's sales rose, as did those of his staff. Mr. Hobbs nodded his approval, which was a lot coming from him. Martin took the time to observe from a different perspective the advertising of his competitors.

Once again at NR's, Martin spoke of what he was learning with Jen and she shared with him a shopping experience she had that day. He hung onto every word she said.

Jen: "I went to the mall today. It wasn't the zoo that is usually is, which was nice. So I went into a store because they had a 'no tax' sale on. Well, it seems that the 'no tax' is on 'select items'. I'm telling you, that kind of stuff really gets me going. If you're going to advertise something, then be clear with me because I thought the whole store was 'no tax'."

Martin: "Why is this such a big deal to you?"

Jen: "Martin, I walked up to the till with 3 items, all of which they charged the tax on. I thought they were going to discount the tax before they swiped my credit card."

Martin: "They didn't?"

Jen: "No! That's when I said something and they said, 'Oh it's no tax for select items only'. I was so embarrassed. I thought for a quick second and then cancelled my order. I wasn't going to be tricked into buying something at a price that is more than I expected to pay. I left there absolutely furious!"

Martin: "Hmmm. I think I need to reflect on this a little."

Another Cup of Wisdom

Back at the coffee shop, which was feeling like a second office if not a classroom for Martin, Nic had a seat with a frothy non-fat latté. Martin told Nic the events of Jen's shopping experience. Nic was amused.

Martin: "What's so funny?"

Nic: "Hey. It sounds like you learned something."

Martin: "Yeah, how NOT to do business. Jen will probably never go into that store again."

Nic: "That's probably true for you and me too now. See the impact? That's Boutique Thinking!"

Martin: "Totally!"

Nic: "There are a variety of places to learn how to improve one's self and business. We just need to be aware. Take this place for example. We're regulars, they treat us great don't they?"

Martin: "Love the extra foam!"

Nic: "Exactly. And you don't ask for it anymore, they just do it for you. In that, lies the lesson."

Martin: "Which is?"

Nic, smiling: "The world is your school … and your play-ground."

Martin: "I like that. So basically every time I have a transaction outside of my work is an opportunity to learn."

23

Nic: "You're really good my man!"

Martin: "Learning from one of the best!"

Nic: "Thanks. Then take the learning to the next level of Boutique Thinking and act upon it. Make a list of places where you have transactions outside of work that are learning opportunities. The reason I suggest the list is that you will become consciously connected to your goals."

Martin was already writing: "Got it. I'm going to get a refill. Can I get you one?"

Nic: "Love one! Can I recommend a book?"

Martin: "You bet!"

Nic: "Go pick up Purple Cow by Seth Godin."

"The world is your school ... and your playground."

Out of Office Learning

Write a list of examples where you can now be "consciously" aware of learning opportunities:

By being "consciously" aware of these learning opportunities, you are literally focused on your success. Every time you look and learn you increase your chances of success.

_____

_____

_____

_____

_____

_____

_____

_____

_____

_____

_____

_____

Back Up

Nic walked into the store with a couple of steaming coffees to find Martin stepping away from his clients on the floor and answering a phone call. Once he was done on the call Martin jumped back in to the conversation with his customers, aware that Nic was watching.

Then the phone rang.
Off to answer it was Martin.

For the 3rd call, Nic took initiative. Martin turned towards the phone at which point he noticed Nic with a raised hand waving him back to the clients on the floor.

Nic took the call and acquired the name and return number of the query. For the next 10 minutes, Martin was allowed to focus on what he did best.

After Martin rang up the sale, he looked at Nic, smiled & said: "Thanks for your help!"

Nic: "No problem. Now the pop quiz."

Martin: "Pop quiz?"

Nic: "Yup! What did you learn over the last 20 minutes?"

Martin reflected about this & said: "That I can sell under pressure?"

Nic: "Actually, no you can't."

Martin: "But I just closed that deal."

Nic: "Because I gave you the "back up" you needed to focus on the customers needs. How many times did the phone ring?"

Martin: "Lots."

Nic: "Imagine if I had the servers in my restaurants answering the phones. How would your service be?"

Martin: "Hmm. Good point."

Nic: "Adding back up to your team allows you all to focus on your skills that make the boutique model run, not sputter."

Martin: "I'm not sure I follow you 100%."

Nic: "That's brave of you to admit. Glad you can do that.
OK. In this case, I'd suggest you hire a cashier or reception person. This allows you & your sales staff to do what you do best: serve your customers."

"Back up allows you to do what you do best: Serve your customers."

Martin: "I got it."

Nic: "I also suggest that you train your back-up personnel to have purpose. In your case, they are the liaison between an in-coming call and an appointment with the appropriate customer advisor."

Martin: "Nice! I like that: Customer Advisor."

Nic: "The training that back up personnel acquires becomes a stepping-stone for their growth in the company. How to answer the phone and have customers be enticed to coming in the store is a big deal. In fact, if you have someone who doesn't have good phone skills, it could really hurt your business."

Martin: "What do you mean?"

Nic: "If you encounter someone who put you on hold too often or for too long, how do you feel? How about someone who isn't pleasant with you?"

Martin: "Good point."

Nic: "This alone is way bigger than people think. Encountering great phone skills could mean the sale being assured before the client is even in the door! A 'back up team' is your support team and they will allow you to serve your clients at the highest levels."

Martin: "Come to think of it, I always tell Jen how *impressed* I am with the people on the end of the line from the Gourmet Pizza Parlor we always order from."

Nic: "Diane's?"

Martin: "Yeah! You know it?"

Nic: "Best Pizza in town!"

Save It & Use It

Martin: "I'm trying my first Americano."

Nic: "Enjoy."

After some sipping Nic got down to business: "So what did you think of the last book?"

Martin: "It was awesome! The only problem is that it inspired me with too many ideas."

Nic: "I love when that happens. Inspired comes from "in spirit". When you tap into that energy, you have to harness it Martin."

"When you tap into Inspiration, you have to harness it."

Martin: "I'd love to live there!"

Nic: "I think everyone wants to in one way or another my friend. The key is follow thru. Take advantage of this in all your interactions because it all comes back to you. That's the balance piece."

Martin: "How do I hang onto all these ideas? I mean, sometimes my brain just starts to fire them off like a baseball pitching machine gone wild!"

Nic: "OK, OK. Here's where you start.
"Confucius say: Bad handwriting better than good memory."

Martin: "I like that."
Nic: "Good. It gets even better. Carry one these with you."

Nic proceeds to show his palm organizer: "This little guy is my "extra brain". It allows my mind to calm down because I've committed my ideas to writing. You can carry around a pad and pen; this is way easier to organize."

Martin: "Can't run away from technology can we?"

Nic: "Embrace it my friend, or lose the race. In no time at all you'll find it easy and actually liberating."

Martin: "Sounds reasonable. I've been thinking about getting one."

Nic: "You'll wonder what you've done without it!"

Martin: "OK. Now I've got my ideas written down. Now what?"

Nic: "A wise man once told me: "You can do anything you want. You just can't do everything you want.""

Martin: "A mentor perhaps?"

Nic: "Bingo!"

Martin: "So what do I do?"

Nic: "Take your list and let your ideas … percolate for a while. Like a few days. Especially if you're not sure what level of priority you want to give them."

"Let your ideas percolate for a while."

Martin: "Percolate. I like that."

Nic: "So will your mind. Stay focused on your current project. If an idea comes along that is a great addition and not extra baggage to the cause, then bring it on. If it does not work with the current task at hand, save it for later."

Martin: "I've had so many things pull me in different directions."

Nic: "That won't ever stop happening to a person like you Martin. You have that energy people want to harness. Just make sure that what ever it is you choose to take on next, it works with what your personal mantra is all about. That alone can help keep you in the right direction."

Martin: "Hmmm. Sounds like work smarter not harder."

Nic: "Well done my friend! Take this with you."

Nic handed Martin the book Rich Dad Poor Dad by Robert Kiyosaki.

Nic: "Now get moving! I'll see you in a couple weeks."

Building Momentum

Over the next coffee meeting Martin was thrilled with his progress and was assured by a recent meeting with Mr. Hobbs that things had really turned around. "What ever you're doing kid, I like it. Keep it up!"

Nic: "Positive feedback from the boss? My word! There is a God!"

Martin: "Yeah. It's cool that I'm in the good books again. Now my dilemma is getting more customers thru the door.
Mr. Hobbs won't increase the advertising budget."

Nic smiled: "So what's the problem?"

Martin: "How am I going to increase sales if I don't get more traffic?"

Nic: "Who told you that your traffic flow is based solely on your advertising budget?"

Martin: "History."

Nic: "History? History is exactly that, in the past. What you need is to focus on NOW."

Martin: "OK ... You've lost me."

Nic: "Everything that is happening NOW is a result of the actions of the past. If you are unhappy with the current state of traffic right now, you can't go change the past."

"Everything that is happening NOW is a result of the actions of the past."

Martin: "OK. That's fair. What can I do now for better traffic in the future?"

Nic: "You frequent NR's?"

Martin: "Yeah, you know that. Regularly I might add."

Nic just smiled that big smile of his.
For Martin it was another electrical storm in his head.

Nic: "What keeps you coming back?"

Martin: "Value of the product and the atmosphere, the energy of the place. Jen loves the attention she gets from NR's at home with the cards you send us."

Nic: "She loves the attention eh? Then it's working!"

Martin: "Your marketing?"

Nic: "Better than that: The Positive Energy Martin; Boutique Thinking Energy. That's my goal. AND that's your goal."

Nic: "Focus on what you are good at and let everyone know how good you are at it. Now go pick up the book Discover Your Sales Strengths by Smith & Rutigliano."

Martin: "I'm on it."

The Boutique Boom
(It's bigger than you think)

The latest meeting was a "red-eye" as Nic called it. 7AM sharp with double doubles. (Twice the sugar, twice the cream.)

Nic: "Let's get down to business shall we?"

Martin: "Let's."

Nic: "So what's the long term plan for you Martin?"

Martin: "What do you mean?"

Nic: "You've made huge changes over the last short while with excellent results. You're turning Mr. Hobbs' store around. Let me rephrase the question: Can a guy like you ever be done?"

Martin: "You must have spy equipment in your restaurants. Jen & I were just talking about the future and what challenges I want to tackle next."

Nic: "So?"

Martin: "Well, I think I deserve a raise."

Nic with a touch of sarcasm: "You think?"

Martin: "I'd like to speak to Mr. Hobbs about it."

Nic: "I think you should too. The sooner the better. You're a valuable asset to his team. A *Partner* in fact."

Martin: "I like the sound of that."

Nic: "You should. You deserve it."

Martin: "Are you suggesting I talk to Mr.Hobbs about becoming a partner?"

Nic: "It's an option. It depends on how comfortable you both are with each other. One thing's for sure, you've proven yourself and you have nothing to lose. If it's something you want, ask."

Martin: "I'd love it. I just don't think he'd go for it."

Nic: "Aren't you in sales? How do you know if you don't ask?"

"How do you know if you don't ask?"

Martin: "I don't have enough money to buy half."

Nic: "Who said anything about half? Just ASK."

Martin: "Ah. This is a listening skills test. I got it."

Nic: "Very good Grasshopper. Maybe Mr. Hobbs would be prepared to part with a smaller share of the business."

Martin: "What kind of percentage?"

Nic: "That's up to you to find out."

Martin: "I can see what's in it for me: Ownership, building equity, and a stake in an industry I enjoy. What's in it for Mr. Hobbs?"

Nic: "A valuable partner, an owner operator more committed to the success of the enterprise and a profitable exit strategy or a passive income stream."

Martin: "Sounds really good for him too."

Nic: "If you start a conversation with him, you could certainly ask him what his future plans are. What is his *Exit Strategy*?"

Martin: "What is your exit strategy?"

Nic: "Merger & acquisitions of good companies are inevitable in today's age of publicly traded companies. The problem for the really big companies is they can't have the flexibility of the small guy. The Boutique Thinkers are stealth and agile whereas the Big Box is very slow to react."

"Boutique Thinkers are stealth and agile."

Martin: "OK."

Nic: "The large conglomerate can offer something to the Boutique though: Marketing, growth, a large profit and eventually a retirement plan & legacy. The Boutique becomes a part of the Big Box "portfolio" AND REMAINS a Boutique. That's the rub."

Martin: "That actually happens?"

Nic: "More than ever my young apprentice. Next time you are enjoying a "micro-brewed" beer at NR's, take a look at the fine print and you'll note that a major company owns that Boutique Thinker."

Martin: "Wow. So you want to sell you NR restaurants?"

Nic: "If the deal is right for me and my team, sure."

Martin: "Just like that? Sell them off and walk away from all the work you put into them?"
Nic: "It would depend on what comes up. It has to be the right deal. You know I have several locations right?"

Martin: "Yeah."

Nic: "Well what you don't know is that the last 3 locations, I've partnered with the on-site management teams to ensure them a start in ownership and me some strong accountability partners."

Martin: "Now that is smart."

Nic: "Absolutely. It provides me with leverage, and passive income."

Martin: "Sweet!"

Nic smiling: "Very sweet."

Martin reflected for a moment: "So my senses tell me that you are suggesting I present this idea to Mr. Hobbs."

Nic: "Or something like it."

Martin: "You have other options?"

Nic: "There are always options. You have a dream?"

Martin: "Yes!"

Nic: "Then keep thinking about it. Feel it and live it!"

Nic then magically made appear yet another book. The book was called, The Tipping Point by Malcolm Gladwell. Martin just laughed and shook his mentor's hand and headed to the cashier.

Boutique Inventory And Leverage

Martin was surprised to receive an email from Nic, telling him the next meeting was at 8AM in a warehouse district of an industrial park. He was very curious and looked forward to meeting his mentor.

When Martin arrived, he was even more surprised to see Nic and another man standing in front of Nic's car sharing coffee. Nic waved hello to Martin with thermos in hand.

Martin: "Ah, coffee! You are good Nic."

Nic: "Thanks my friend. Martin I'd like for you to meet a friend of mine, Casey James."

Martin: "Nice to meet you Casey."

Casey: "Pleasure's mine. We've been hearing about you at work."

Martin looked puzzled.

Nic: "Casey is my top kitchen manager, and we talk a lot."

Martin: "All good I hope!"

Casey smiling: "All good man. You really lucked with this guy in your corner. (Casey pointed his mug of coffee towards Nic). He's taught many of us the value of giving back. That's why I'm here."

Martin looked at Nic: "What's up"?

Nic smiled: "Well my friend, I figured it was time to discuss the concept of Boutique Thinking inventory controls."

Martin: "I thought we went over that already in to book you recommended I read a few weeks ago."

Nic: "It's ongoing my friend."

Casey: "Kaizen!"

Martin chuckled: "OK. Bring it on!"

Nic: "Any guess as to what brings us to this warehouse area?"

They were standing in front of a specialty butcher shop.

Martin: "Not a clue."

Nic: "This principle is going to be even more important for you than for me Martin."

Martin: "OK."

Casey: "Nic gave me the heads up with how he's been helping you. He taught me this lesson a few years ago and that's why I'm here."

Martin now very curious: "Taught you what?"

Casey: "Come with me my new friend."

At that moment, Nic's phone rang: "I'll take this & I'll be with you guys in a minute."

Casey: "No sweat."

Martin followed Casey into the building. Nic stayed outside to take his call.

Casey began as they walked down the hall: "Nic has taught many of us to be a team. We rely on each other when we can."

Martin: "Makes sense."

Casey: "He's a master at getting things done, and he's actually teaching the both of us that we don't have to go it alone."

Martin: "What do you mean?"

Casey smiling: "Two for the price of one today."

Martin felt puzzled.
They walked to the reception area.

Casey: "Hello Val."

Val, the receptionist: "Hey Casey."

Casey: "Can you let Jackie know I'm here?"

Val: "She knows. She's just finishing a call and she'll be right out."

Casey: "Thanks."

Casey and Martin sat down on very comfortable leather couches. The reception area wasn't very large, yet the decor was clearly about one thing: Meat.

Casey: "OK. The 2 in 1 thing I mentioned earlier is Nic knew he was going to have an important phone call that he couldn't reschedule. He knew I was coming here, so he asked me to give you a mentor's touch, from an industry outside your own."

Martin: "OK."

Casey: "Well Martin. That's the first of 2."

Martin: "OK I'm lost."

Casey: "Nic just leveraged himself by asking me to give a lesson while he had to take a call."

Martin: "Leverage."

Casey: "Give me a lever long enough and I can move the world."

Martin: "I've heard that before"

Casey: "Good. It's a good saying and Nic is putting it to action."

Martin: "So the first thing is: it's OK to ask for other people's help."

"It's OK to ask for other people's help."

Casey: "Absolutely! Otherwise you end up micro managing and doing a lot less by yourself."

Martin: "Smart guy."

Casey: "Here comes Jackie."

Out of her office came a woman dressed in business casual with a white butchers coat draped over her arm.

Casey: "Jackie Greenwood, this a very good friend of Nic Robinson's, Martin Sparks."

Martin: "Pleasure to meet you."

Jackie: "Nice to meet you Martin. I have to give credit to Nic, Casey."

Casey: "What for?"

Jackie: "He's a great model for me. I've been helping a kid from a junior high school and it's been very rewarding. Is he here?"

Casey: "He's just outside on a call. He'll catch up."

Jackie looked at Martin then at Casey and smiled: "Ah, leverage."

Martin was blown away that she had the lesson pegged.

Jackie: "You're not the first guy Casey brings along for an inventory tour Martin."

Martin: "Oh. I get it now."

Casey smiled: "So, how we doing in the bison department?"

Jackie: "Follow me guys and put one of these on."

Jackie pointed to a rack of white coats.
Martin and Casey each slipped into their respective coats and followed Jackie towards the meat hanging & storage area.

Casey: "Although I manage the kitchens for NR's, I occasionally like to visit with my suppliers rather than them always coming to me."

Jackie: "I don't have many clients come to visit. What I do know is Nic & Casey care about the quality of the goods we supply them with."

Casey: "And the quantity and availability."

Martin, who was a little cold in the meat locker: "So what does this have anything to do with what Nic mentioned earlier? How is this marketing?"

Nic: "Boutique Inventory AND Marketing, Martin."

Everyone was surprised to see Nic at the entrance of the locker.

Jackie: "You scared me!"

Nic: "Great to see you Jackie. Sorry about that."

Jackie: "It's OK. You sure know how to make an entrance."

They all laughed.

Nic: "Martin, Casey has to know what is coming down the pipeline when it comes to availability, and he needs to keep me informed."

Martin: "This way you know what to promote during the week."

Casey: "He catches on fast."

Nic with pride: "He certainly does. Jackie is also an integral part of our team. As a supplier, if she knows that she will be having a shortage on her Bison, then I know to inform the location managers, who will inform the kitchen and serving staff to not promote the Bison in wild blueberry reduction sauce."

Jackie: "Lucky for all of us, I make sure that my supply is steady because that's one of my favorite dishes!"

Casey: "Anyone involved in your business must be regarded as a team player."

Nic: "Well said Casey. Ultimately, when your whole team gels together, Boutique Thinking Principles thrive."

"When your whole team gels together, Boutique Thinking Principles thrive."

After a tour of the operation, Casey, Martin and Nic said their respective good-byes to Jackie and returned to the bookstore for a recommendation and another coffee.

Arrive Early

It was time for the morning "pick me up" for Nic and Martin. Nic was already there waiting for Martin who arrived right at 8:00AM.

Nic: "At 8:01 I was going to start to worry."

Martin sarcastically. "You? Worry?"

Nic smiled: "Arriving on time is good. It is expected and acceptable. Just remember, an expectation is a resentment in hiding. Arriving early is always better."

Martin: "What do you mean? Did I do something wrong?"

Nic, laughing now: "No! I'm just giving you some advice my friend. It's like our meeting right now. We agreed that 8:00AM was when we'd meet. You arrived at 8:00AM, no problem."

Martin: "OK."

Nic: "The reason I asked for us to meet at 8:00 instead of 9:00 is because I'm helping at my daughters' school today and I don't want to be late. Can you imagine my little girl at
9:01 if I'm still not there?"

Martin: "Hmm. I never thought of it like that."

Nick: "Here's another Boutique Thinking lesson. Think of every appointment like you are applying for a job. Do you remember applying for your first job as a teen?"

Martin smiling: "Yes I do."
Nic: "Let me guess; you were very early."

Martin: "Was I that obvious?"

Nic: "Not really. The fact is, when you really want something, you put extra energy into it."

"Think of every appointment like you are applying for a job."

Martin: "I guess I got you a little nervous then?"

Nic: "Not at all Martin. I just wanted to mention a value that many customers, including yours, will appreciate."

Martin: "Noted!"

Nic: "Excellent. For your next book, I'm going to recommend Authentic Leadership by Bill George."

Value Your Network

Martin and Nic got down to business right away. This time armed with double shot lattés.

Nic: "One of the things I've been striving for all along, no matter how many locations I open, is to keep my values and those of my team on the same page."

Martin: "What do you mean?"

Nic: "There are certain establishments that people frequent regularly, not because it's cheap, but because of the way they feel when they are there."

"People frequent certain businesses because of the way they feel."

Martin: "Personal Care! Part of Boutique Thinking of course."

Nic, proud of his pupil: "Exactly! In the same breath, that energy is sent back to the people who work in the establishment. Employees become team members. In the remarkable businesses, team members AND regular customers CHANGE to something else."

Martin: "Change? To What?"

Nic, now smiling: "They become *family*. Better yet, they become your *friends*! That's the essence of a boutique. Can you really "feel like family" in a big box store?"

Martin thought about this for a moment: "I can't. You're right. I'm getting it. But it still doesn't help me with increasing my numbers at the store right now."

Nic: Let's consider the friends you've made then.

Rely On Who And What You Know

Nic: "Do you have a database?"

Martin: "Yeah."

Nic: "Do you know what that database is for?"

Martin paused … "Yes. To keep in touch with our clients."

Nic in his classic sarcastic tone: "So?"

Martin: "I have some work ahead of me."

Nic smiling now: "Sounds like it. Stay focused, and we'll catch up later."

What ensued over the next 2 weeks was Martin putting together an action plan for Mr. Hobbs' first ever Friends & Family Sale.

Martin took every free second he had to go over the database, all the way back to the *handwritten* invoices from when the company first started, what seemed like eons ago.
Martin then got in touch with the post office and found out what the details were on a direct mailer to his database. He then went over his e-mail list and devised an e-mail to contact his clients about the sale.

Relation = Elation

20 days to go before the sale and Martin is once again meeting with Nic for some jet fuel for his body and his mind. With 2 high-octane lattes, they got down to business.

Nic: "So what have you done to draw people in?"

Martin went over his list:
    -"Well, I've gone over the WHOLE client list, even the written invoices, and sent out a huge mailer telling people about the sale."
    -"I then sent out a broadcast e-mail to those people whose e-mail address we have on file."

Nic: "That's good. Go on."

Martin: "I took the old written invoice clients & added them to our electronic database."

Nic: "I would expect that from you at this point. Good move."

Martin: "I'm missing something. I can tell by the way you're talking. What?"

Nic: "You're learning Martin. Go with your gut like that more often and you'll go farther than you can imagine."

Martin: "OK. My gut tells me you have something big in store for me. That there's more I can do to make this event successful."

Nic smiled a big smile: "OK Martin. With all the advertising in the world, does that ensure you are going to have the traffic & more importantly the quality customer you are looking for to come to this *event?*"

Martin, now feeling dejected: "No…. So has all the intense work I've put into this thing been all for nothing?"

Nic: "Not at all! You've been competing with the same rules & tools as the big box guys. You now have to take your game to the boutique level."

"Take your game to the Boutique level."

Nic: "How many friends would you say you have Martin?"

Martin: "I have a lot. Only a few I would call best friends."

Nic: "It feels good to have friends doesn't it? They are a resource we count on when we need them."

Martin: "Sure. It seems I'm everyone's best friend when they are moving because I have a pick-up truck!"

Nic laughed: "The road you're now on is a way towards having your clients or "friends" realize that you are a valuable resource and that they can come to you to help them build a better quality of life through the services & products you provide."

Nic continued: "I call this the Relation: Elation principle. I believe it is our goal to have our friends and clients be elated to visit us. Friends are loyal. We are creating that with our continued goal to help them, to be genuine, to be value driven and to be centered on our principles.

"Are your clients elated to visit you?"

Martin: "Relation/Elation. OK. So what am I missing?"

Nic: "The tide is moving to a place where our clients are wiser & are growing on the inside. People have a stronger sense of themselves and what they like. With this wisdom, comes the ability to sense when someone or even a company someone works for is not authentic. The paying customer can sense the good, the bad and the ugly."

"People can <u>sense</u> the good, the bad and the ugly."

Martin: "That makes sense. Especially because my target audience is getting older, I would hope they get wiser."

Nic: "We're all getting wiser my friend. We are learning from our experiences. That is why the personal touch is so important."

Martin: "So how can I add this "personal touch" when I still have a business to run?"

Nic: "That's a great question. Meet me here tomorrow morning, same time."

Personalize Your Message

Martin walked into the mentorship office (the coffee shop/bookstore) to find Nic speaking with a woman. Nic was taking notes. On the table were also 3 cups and one pot of coffee.

Nic: "Ah Martin, I'd like for you to meet Tracy Dempsey."

Martin: "Nice to meet you."

TD: "The pleasure is all mine Martin. I've heard a lot about you."

Martin: "You have?" Martin looked at Nic.

Nic smiled: "Martin, TD is a friend and valuable mentor of mine."

Martin surprised: "Oh. Well I'm really pleased to meet you!"

TD smiling: "Thanks."

Nic: "TD & I meet once in while to bounce ideas off each other. I learn a TON from this woman."

TD: "Nic, without your valuable information I wouldn't be as far ahead as I am. I am very grateful for you male insights."

Nic & TD clinked their coffee cups like a couple old pals in a pub without spilling a drop.

Martin in his fun sarcastic tone: "Hmmm. I feel a lesson coming on here."

Both Nic & TD laughed.
TD: "He's funny and intuitive!"

Nic: "He sure is. You're right Martin. Both TD & I realized years ago that to understand any great mystery, you must study as many aspects as possible."

Martin: "OK."

Nic: "Half of the people we do business with are …"

Martin looked right into TD's eyes: "Women!"

TD: "You're a master at stating the obvious there Martin."

Martin laughing: "Thanks."

Nic: "The point is I have a few close peers that are men and others are women and I do that on purpose."

TD: "I do the same Martin."

Martin was spinning now and he was totally getting the picture.

TD: "I take it you & Nic discussed who your customer is?"

Martin: "Yes."

TD: "In your case Martin, how many of your customers are women?"

Martin: "About 60%."

TD: "That's over half your client base."

Nic was just sitting & smiling knowing what was coming next.
TD: "Out of all you clients Martin, who makes the buying decision?"

It was like a blinding light for Martin: "Aw. Man is she good!"

Nic burst out laughing: "She's on our team buddy!"

TD: "May I suggest something to you Martin?"

Martin: "Sure!"

TD: "Nic has helped me a great deal to think more and more like a boutique owner. The "care package" I've put together makes a point of recognizing Women as vital to the growth of my business interests."

"Recognize women as vital to the growth of your business."

Martin: "That makes sense. What are some aspects of your "Care package?""

TD: "The heart of it is what I understand you and Nic spoke of yesterday. The Personal Touch."

Martin: "I'm glad you are bringing this up."

Nic: "That's why she's here pal."

TD: "Beyond the physical differences between men and women, there are a few things from an emotional stand point that also set us apart."

Martin: "I'll agree with you there."

TD: "That being the case, the Boutique Thinkers that appeal to us will win us over BIG TIME."

TD pulls out her laptop: "Check this out."

She punches in: www.sendoutcards.com

Martin: "What's this?"

Nic: "This is awesome."

TD: "This Martin, is my secret weapon against the Big Box. From this site, I send my customers custom cards."

Martin: "Like an e-card? That's not new or innovative."

TD: "Hang on Martin. It's NOT an e-card. This is where I send a REAL card. I select it and "customize it". They print it, stuff it, stamp it and send it out for me."

Martin: "Wow. That's pretty cool."

TD: "It's very cool. I can take a of picture you and Nic, then upload it to a card and say 'thanks' and even include a gift card for this coffee shop inside."

Martin: "Now that I like!"

Nic: "I told you it was awesome."

TD: "See, when I get an e-card, it's nice, but then I delete it."

Nic: "That's exactly what most customers do as well. You're even lucky if they actually open the e-mail."

TD: "Did you know that the average consumer receives 3000 commercial messages a day?"

Martin: "Wow! That's a lot of marketing and waste."

TD: "Right. With this service my clients are raving because they get the "personal touch" in a place where they expect to find a bill, instead they are finding a 'surprise'! When was the last time you got a surprise in the mail?"

Martin was blown away: "This is amazing. Is it expensive?"

TD: "It's way cheaper than buying cards at a store! AND it is extremely convenient."

Nic: "Remember the 80/20 rule?"

Martin: "For sure."

Nic: "You have to *really* take care of your customers that make up your 20%. I've been implementing it for NR's; the personal touch is the way to go."

Martin: I'm a Boutique Thinker too! How do I get set up to do this?

Tracy went over the details with Martin and Nic. Martin was now armed better than ever to set himself and his business apart from the Big Box.

80/20 + Leverage

The next meeting was an evening. This was out of the ordinary but Nic had something come up with his kids and asked Martin to switch their time to 8:00PM. Martin was early so he took his steaming latte and perused the books. Nic arrived early as well and decided to have a cup of house blend and then invited Martin to sit down.

Nic: "Remember the 80/20 Rule?"

Martin: "Yeah."

Nic: "OK", he pauses for effect. Martin then feels a vibration in his pants. He almost jumps out of his chair. His phone just received a text.
Martin reaches into his pocket for his phone and finds a text from Nic with a "smiley" on it.

Martin looks up at him: "Nice one."

Nic laughing: "Thanks."

Martin: "Is this a hint?"

Nic: "Yes it is."

Martin: "OK. Based on the 80/20 rule, 80 percent of my total store sales come from 20 percent of my inventory."

Nic: "Where else does this rule apply?"

Martin: "To my sales force. I have one guy who hits home runs while the others are hit and miss."

Nic: "That's true in most businesses. Good training changes that though, right?"

Martin: "I'll admit it, it does. I've seen the changes in my numbers and once my team really gets in on it, I can only imagine."

Nic: "Excellent. So where else can the 80/20 apply?"

Martin paused: "My targets! I also have a percentage of regular and big-ticket clients that would probably be about 20% of my client base!"

Nic, sipping and smiling: "M-hmm."

Martin: "And based on the sneaky smiley move to my phone, I am to call or directly contact these people?"

Nic: "It's the Boutique way my friend. And?"

Martin: "And what?"

Nic: "The personal touch, the Boutique touch."

Martin: "For sure! I'll do the card thing."

Nic: "More than that Martin. Those clients have relationships with certain staff members, right?"

Martin jumped in: "I get it! Now I have to get my team to jump in."

"Get your team to jump in."

Nic: "Exactly. Just because *YOU* think like a Boutique doesn't mean you can't delegate or get your team involved. Boutique Thinking is intimate. Care for your customer begins from the team member who dealt with that customer. Leverage that care. A key factor to Boutique Thinking is having any and all team members be accountable and responsible for the energy sent out."

**"Boutique Thinking
Is about the Energy
you give to each customer"**

Nic continued: "Each staff member is his or her own independent Boutique Brand within the store."

Martin: "That's why they have the incentives, they are the brand."

Nic: "How does your team like the changes since you've started learning and applying more?"

Martin: "Actually, there were a couple of skeptics. The truth is morale has never been better."

Nic: "Excellent. Now you are creating the environment customers *want* to come and deal in. When your client gets that personal touch from the actual person they dealt with, the friend factor takes place, barriers and walls are non-existent."

Martin: "I get it. This is an initiative that should be on-going, not just for a sale."

"The personal touch is an initiative that should be on-going."

Nic: "Exactly! You remember my mentor, Richard Caan?"
Martin: "Absolutely!"

Nic: "Well, my mentor told me that he's had certain businesses that he had stopped soliciting "new" customers because of the level of care that he wanted to provide his existing client base. Know what happened?"

Martin: "I'm not sure."

Nic: "His sales almost doubled."

Martin: "Wow!"

Nic: "That's what happens Martin. Loyalty. Friendship. Care. They are all part of the package. And you're on your way there. Many trainers out there believe that clients can't be your friends. In my experience, the best reps, staff or field agents are the ones that clients LIKE. We are all making good products at a similar price when it comes down to it. Take a step back once in a while and check your values. Believe in your values and yourself and you will succeed."

Martin: "I know I am."

"Loyalty, Friendship, Care: They are all part of the package."

Nic: "That is why the question: "Who is my customer" is so important to define. We must *consistently* market to that client."

Martin: "I'm doing it now."

Nic: "Good. I'm also going to suggest you do it consistently after as well."

Martin: "What do you mean?"

Nic: "The Big Box guys are always marketing the same way. Discounts, sales, price slashing. What they are *saying* to people is they want something from them: Their money. Period."

Martin just leaned in listening intently.

Nic: "The Boutique must market by giving."

Martin: "Giving? What is that going to cost me?"

Nic: "Get out of the big box Martin. Giving doesn't have to cost you anything."

Martin: 'I'd like an example please."

Nic: "No sweat. How about a card that simply says: 'THANK YOU for your trust in us'. No more, no less. Just Thanks. You can send a card or make a call as a follow up weeks or even years later to simply check in and provide your business card and number inside to see if your customer is satisfied or that they are reaching their goal or that you are there to provide more service."

Martin jumped in: "OK I get it. I have to admit, I get caught up in purely the money aspect of it."

Nic: "That's the part you must un-learn my friend. Once you do that, the money rushes in. Call it your demon plan".

Martin: "Demon Plan?"

Nic: "D.M.N. plan actually. Direct Marketing Now. Why market to a whole city when you can focus on the specific neighborhood or better yet those clients who represent your 20% of the 80/20 rule? When consistent, it is a powerful way to market against Big Box. When would now be a good time to start?"

"The D.M.N.: A powerful way to market against Big Box."

Martin: "DMN. That's hot!"

Nic laughed: "Get outta here."

The D.M.N. Plan

List your database:

-Top 20% clients based on total sale or frequency of purchase.

-Based on what you know of your clients. You can also use a map (or Google Earth) and pinpoint where your clients live by zip code. Thus focus on your DMN and crank up the heat!

-By giving the "personalized touch", tools such as Sendoutcards.com become the cornerstone of the Boutique Thinkers DMN plan.

"When would Now be a good time to start?"

Is Price What You're Selling?

The direct marketing plan was on its way. Martin thought "leverage" and his staff followed suit.

Martin and Nic met again for a morning coffee to go over some of the ideas Martin had to entice clients into the store.

Nic: "Are you seriously thinking about competing against Big Box? Here's the deal. If you are contemplating about beating a giant at their own game, you're dead."

Nic could see that Martin had a worried look in his eyes.

Martin: "But everyone wants the lowest price."

Nic: "I'm going to call BS here my friend. Remember the law of attraction? If you advertise lowest price, then everyone coming in will be looking for lowest price."

"If you advertise lowest price, then everyone coming in will be looking for lowest price."

Martin sighing: "OK, you're right."

Nic: "Best price, best quality, best service. You can't have all 3. As a Boutique Thinker who truly cares about what customers are looking for, consider RESULTS as your driving force."

Martin: "We do. But I have to admit we finish all of our ads with something to do with price."

Nic: "If you advertise 'lowest price' just remember that your customers will also become those who leave for the lowest price."

Martin: "They go somewhere else, to a Big Box perhaps?"

Nic: "Exactly. If you advertise best results, you will attract customers who are wanting and needing results. Price does not involve emotions, results do! What are results worth to a customer?"

"Price does not involve emotions, RESULTS DO!"

Nic paused for effect: "Results are worth the investment that you are offering."

"Results are worth the investment that you are offering."

Martin, feeling inspired: "Yes they are!"

Nic: "Now remember what we spoke of weeks ago? Who's your customer?"

Martin: "Yeah."

Nic: "Well, here are facts that can't be denied:
1. Women continue to become a larger market segment.
2. Older people continue to become a larger market segment."

Martin now hesitating: "OK."

Nic: "I just said earlier that price is NOT and emotional option"

Martin: "Yeah I remember."
Nic: "Good. Then remember this: Women tend to be more in touch with their feelings than men are."

"Women tend to be more in touch with their feelings than men are."

Martin chuckling: "Jen says this to me all the time."

Nic: "She's right. And as men, we need to soak it in. Ever read Men are From Mars Women are from Venus?"

Martin: "Let me guess, if I haven't I'm going to?"

Nic: "You catch on quick my friend. Before we leave today, go buy it."

Martin: "Noted!"

Nic: "Good. The reason is this relationship book is also a great business reference."

Martin: "How so?"

Nic: "It explains a lot regarding the way women think and how men think in regards to women."

Martin: "So how did this affect your restaurants?"

Nic: "I'll give you one example then I want you to go read the book and apply what you've learned for yourself."

Martin: "OK."

Nic: "When you go into any NR's location, and you have to use the bathroom you'll note that our bathrooms are exceptionally clean."

Martin: "Clean? They're spotless! Jen keeps saying that the women's bathroom at NR's is like a lounge! She loves it!"

Nic smirking: "Mission accomplished. Here's another great fact: Women tend to discuss their great finds and emotional likes more often than men do. My restrooms have become a marketing tool."

"Women tend to discuss their great finds and emotional likes more often than men do."

Martin stopped and stared at Nic: "Where do I find this book?"

Boutique Thinking is Intimate

It had taken 3 weeks before Martin met Nic for another meeting as it took him some time to read the latest recommended book. With the successful Friends and Family Sale behind him, Martin could continue his growth plans. Proud of his accomplishment, Martin set up the next meeting with Nic for Tuesday at 8:00 AM. When Nic arrived, Martin had a couple of steaming lattes being poured.

Nic: "Wow, now that's service! Thanks!"

Martin: "My pleasure."

Nic: "You're "in the zone" this morning."

Martin: "Sure am. Loved the last book. Very good."

Nic: "You ever notice the best conversations are the ones that you are "engaged" in? Not just waiting for your turn to speak. I mean truly in the moment."

Martin: "Sure. Whenever we meet it's like that. Or when a customer and I just hit it off for example."

Nic: "THAT is Boutique Thinking in Action. That's why my friend Joel says he'll be forever "engaged" to his fiancée. Because the "tendency" is, once married, the "participation" in the relationship and intensity drops."

Martin: "Now you're scaring me."

Nic laughing: "That's not my intention. I'm just sharing an example!"
Martin: "Nice one. Thanks!"

Nic: "OK. How about this? It's like music. Some of the best concerts are the one's where the musicians have an 'intimate & interactive' experience with the audience."

Martin: "Yeah. Those 'unplugged' versions really do offer a more personal perspective."

Nic: "Exactly. Boutique Thinking is about being engaged."

Martin: "Then I'm there!"

Nic: "Yup! Consider Boutique Thinking when applied to Politics. It changes the tables. This is when a candidate is seen as a person and not as a politician."

Martin: "How do we access the intimate factor of Boutique Thinking?"

Nic: "Remember the movie Jerry McGuire? In the end, it is Jerry's Boutique Thinking that makes him a winner. When the care is there, results follow."

"When the Care is there, Results follow."

Thanking Your Customer

A hot coffee during a meeting on a cold morning can soothe the soul. This is the way the meeting with Martin and Nic began one cold morning.

Nic: "Pop quiz. Do you know how often companies truly thank their customer for their business?"

Martin: "I don't know."

Nic: "Almost never."

Martin sarcastically: "I hear a sermon coming on."

Nic burst out laughing: "Alright smart guy."

Martin lifted his coffee and Nic responded with a clinking of cups.

Nic: "Being a Boutique Thinker in a Big Box world requires us to look at the Big Box business model and use what they don't to our advantage."

Martin: "Makes sense."

Nic: "Some of the Big Box guys use "Customer Appreciation" simply as a reason to have a sale or blow out dead inventory. Consumers are smarter then that. If you truly appreciate someone, what do you do?"

Martin: "I'm going to say … Give them something without expecting anything in return."

Nic: "Exactly!"

Martin was surprised: "But what do you give that doesn't make you break your bank? It's not like a small business like mine can afford that."

Nic: "That's a point I knew you'd bring up. Let's look inside the box. What does Big Box do?"

Martin: "For customers? They work on best price, usually."

Nic: "OK. So what can you give?"

Martin, hesitating: "Better service?"

Nic: "You should be already doing that. Come on Martin, what can you give that is priceless?"

Martin: "Information!"

Nic: "Exactly. And not just a tip, I'm talking a whole iceberg. That is what the boutique needs to do to not only separate themselves from Big Box. It is what needs to be done for the Boutique to thrive. You "GIFT" your clients with information. That will continue to build their trust and loyalty."

"Gift your clients with information that Big Box would NEVER provide."

Martin: "How does NR's do that?"

Nic: "Secret Recipes to our VIP clients is a favorite of many of NR's regulars."

Martin: "That's Right! Jen totally digs that."
Nic: "It forces the chefs to continue to push their limits and keep growing their craft. If our menu stayed the same forever, we'd be very Big Box and not Boutique."

Martin: "Makes sense."

Nic: "It has garnered us plenty of loyalty. We also send out cards with cooking tips or wine pairing advice. We also have had closed door events for special clients."

Martin: "Love those cards eh?"

Nic: "They're truly priceless."

Martin: "I think I've got some brainstorming to do."

Nic: "Excellent. Just realize that the information you can provide is probably second nature to you. That's what makes you the expert."

Martin: "So it would obvious to me, but not to my clients."

Nic: "Surprisingly, yes. The affect this has on the people who use this information is awesome. You'll have a walking, talking billboard for your business."

"You'll have a walking, talking billboard for your business."

The GIFT Of Information

What kind of valuable information can your clients use? In most cases, the information I'm speaking of is second nature to you: NOT TO YOUR CUSTOMER.

Put together a list of features and benefits that you think are obvious to your customers.

Make a couple of calls to your loyal client database (your top 20%) and ask them if you can provide them with some feedback regarding an item on your list.

For example: A ski shop owner could assume that "everyone" knows the dos & don'ts of waxing their skis.

A restaurant can provide a wine or beer-pairing seminar.

A hair salon can provide tips on how to style at home between cuts.

Financial planners can put on a "leverage clinic" that is both fun and informative and truly break the mold.

Boutique Hurdles

A frustrated Martin arrived with sweat on his brow for his morning meeting. Nic could feel the energy coming off of Martin. He offered him a latte, which Martin accepted.

Nic: "Let's get down to business shall we?"

Martin nodded.

Nic: "What's going on?"

Martin: "Just feeling stressed."

Nic: "OK."

Martin: "Ideas don't always work the way we think they will."

Nic: "Ah. Expectations are resentments in hiding. So the anger you're letting off is based on what?"

Martin: "Is it that obvious?"

Nic: "Yup."

Martin: "The last couple of days have felt like I'm not getting any quality work done and everything seems to be getting in the way."

Nic: "That's fair. Things happen, and you can be frustrated. Feelings of anger and frustration are normal. Just remember that you are a leader and how you deal with this is what will set you apart."

Martin: "I'll ask you to clarify please."

Nic: "A true Boutique Thinker understands that they may be alone in business AND they are not alone in life. It is OK to be upset or disappointed. The test is: How long do you plan on hanging on to that disappointment? If I hung onto my disappointments I'd be sunk. The only 'appointments' I want are with success."

"The only 'appointments' you want are with success."

Martin: "So what you're saying is I can talk to you about this stuff?"

Nic: "Absolutely! In fact, it is OK to let certain people you work with how you are feeling, as long as you don't rip them apart when telling them."

Martin then let out what he was hanging on to. Nic simply listened. It was just what Martin needed.

Nic: "How do you feel?"

Martin: "You know, I feel 100 times better then when I walked in. Thanks for listening Nic."

Nic smiling: "That's what mentoring is about my friend. Now, I have a movie for you to watch. You'll get a kick out of it. Go rent Boiler Room; you'll see what stress and high pressure in sales is. Take it all with a grain of salt."

Boutique Thinking Success

Martin picked up a couple of extra hot steaming lattés and placed them on the table. It was Martin that caught Nic by surprise this morning.

Martin: "Let's get down to business shall we?"

Nic laughed: "Let's!"

Martin: "Question for you. What are some of the biggest challenges that a Boutique Thinker goes through?"

Nic: "There can be obstacles."

Martin: "Such as?"

Nic: "One of the biggest problems that occur with businesses is the focus of their thinking changes. Ever hear the quote: I think therefore I Am.?"

Martin: "Sure."

Nic: "That doesn't mean that because you think you exist.
It means you are what you think! A Boutique Thinker is focused on helping the customer. A Big Box thinker is only focused on making money."

"You are what you Think."

Martin: "What's wrong with making money?"

Nic: "Nothing! In fact if we didn't make money in our endeavors then it would be difficult to measure our success."

Martin: "Then money is not bad."

Nic: "I never said making money was bad Martin. I'm saying being focused on *only* making money isn't Boutique Thinking."

Martin: "What's the difference?"

Nic: "Making lots of money is a by-product of Boutique Thinking. Focus your energy on the Care that a Boutique Thinker puts into their business, with a barometer of success being money, and you will succeed. When your energy is truly connected to care for a customer, you create a continuous sense of elevation."

"Making Money is a by-product of Boutique Thinking."

Martin: "Elevation? What do you mean?"

Nic: "Have you ever helped a customer purchase what they wanted or needed?"

Martin: "Sure. Thanks to the stuff I'm learning, especially about myself. I'm doing it more and more."

Nic: "Exactly. Now, do you think your customers are happy to make the decision to buy from you?"

Martin: "Of course they are, otherwise they wouldn't."

Nic: "How do you feel knowing that you've truly helped them out and are getting paid well for that?"

Martin: "I understand what you mean by elevated feeling now. I feel great when I help and profit!"

Nic slowly and deliberately: "Then use your mind and think. Use your values and feel. Use that energy and prosper."

Martin was writing that down.

Nic: "Success is not an entitlement. It has to be earned every day."

"Success is not an entitlement.
It has to be earned every day."

Nic: "Want an example?"

Martin: "Sure!"

Nic: "I have a friend of mine who owns a physical performance centre. Now some people would call this a gym or health club or personal training studio. Jeff calls it a physical performance centre and is so focused on helping his clients reach their best athletic potential that he interviews THEM before he decides to take them on as a client."

Martin: "What do you mean?"

Nic: "He's not your average packed health club. I mean, I've heard him turn away people who have the money to pay, but in Jeff's eyes they are not the kind of client who would commit to his programs. So he sends them to a club or a personal training studio suited to that persons needs."

Martin: "Doesn't that cost him money?"

Nic: "No way! In fact what it does is it increases his success ratio. You see, Jeff has one of the best track records for successful training for pro and amateur athletes around. Pros from all over North America fly-in to see him and his team for advice on training and sport related injury rehab and prevention. He gained his excellent reputation by bringing on committed clients who want to succeed as much as he does."

Martin: "Sounds like he took some advice from someone I know."

Nic smiling behind his cup of coffee: "Maybe."

Martin: "He must have some tough programs."

Nic: "Not everyone is prepared to do the work that Jeff would outline. That is why Jeff interviews potential prospects. He doesn't "need" the money. Trust me, when I was training for my triathlon, I paid big dollars to have Jeff on my team."

Martin: "You do Triathlons?"

Nic: "Yeah. I started doing them 11 years ago. Last year, Jeff agreed to help me with my preparation."

Martin: "How'd you do?"

Nic: "I crushed my personal best time by 22 minutes! My best time was 9 years ago and I surpassed it by 22 minutes!"

Martin: "Good for you!"

Nic: "And for Jeff! Now I tell everyone about how great a trainer Jeff is. He wasn't cheap AND the results were worth it."

Martin: "So knowing who your customer is and what you want to do for them is important."

Nic: "You got it. Boutique Thinking is understanding that there are customers out there you DON'T WANT. Jeff knows that. He wants clients who are ready to commit to the hard work."

Martin: "Mr. Hobbs would blow a gasket if I turned away business."

Nic: "Don't be so sure Martin. If a potential customer came in, was negative, was relentless for getting a better price, wanted stuff for free and demanded delivery of his goods at an unreasonable time, would you want his business?"

Martin: "Well, I wouldn't. I've had customers like that. When anything can go wrong, it does! Then they want a new product, or they want a huge in-store credit. But I still think Mr. Hobbs would want their business."

Nic: "Mr. Hobbs will understand if you put things into perspective for him. Tough customers exist. You will have to do business with some. On very rare occasions, you will do yourself and the store a huge favor by offering the difficult client alternative options outside your walls."

Martin: "You think I'd be doing the store a favor?"

Nic: "You will not be forced to change delivery schedules. You don't submit to discounting your excellent products and services and you save yourself from any potential bombardment of negative energy later. This saves you time and money. I'm sure you and Mr. Hobbs have had customers that cost you money."

Martin: "Yes we have!"
Nic: "Are there many of this type of customer?"

Martin: "Not really."

Nic: "The truth is, they are rare. People tend to hang on to the memory of the bad customer for some reason. Boutique Thinking reminds us that we have to let those negative thoughts go."

Martin: "Sounds like I should let those negative customers go as well."

Nic: "That's EXACTLY what you have to do."

Martin: "I was kidding."

Nic: "Well I'm not my friend. What this does for your company is set standards. Mr. Hobbs has certain standards and so do you. It's probably in your best interest to discuss this kind of scenario with him ahead of time, before he walks in and simply sees you offering a client an alternate store."

Martin: "Good idea."

Boutique Thinking: Big Results

Nic: "How's your coffee?"

Martin: "Very good, as always."

Nic: "Ever notice how well they do here?"

Martin: "Are you kidding? The place is always lined up. It's packed."

Nic: "Yup! And we are paying an above average price for the coffee."

Martin: "Yeah, but it's a treat."

Nic: "It is. These guys get Boutique Thinking."

Martin: "But they're huge. Doesn't that mean they are the Big Box?"

Nic: "They are huge. They got that way with Boutique Thinking. The Big Box isn't the enemy. The Big Box is what it is. BIG."

Martin: "It's obviously working for them."

Nic: "These guys are big AND they use Boutique Thinking to their advantage to provide customer care. Do you know how many locations they have?"

Martin: "How many?"

Nic: "Over 13 000 locations and growing…. fast! They're an example of Boutique Thinking in a Big Box World."

Martin: "Holy cow!"

Nic: "Yeah. That's what Boutique Thinking can get you. These guys have it. They've been in business for some time and they continually refine the formula, but the thinking method is consistent."

Martin: "Refine the formula. Kind of like finding that perfect blend of coffee."

Nic: "You got it. And obviously, so do they. As customers, we know they are making good money on the coffee and we still pay the price. They are not just selling coffee."

Martin: "I know the answer to this: They are selling the whole coffee experience."

Nic smiled and stared at his friend: "You got it kid! I come in here and I learn with every cup."

At that moment, another light turned on in Martin's mind.

Martin: "Nic, what is the "essence" of Boutique Thinking?"

Nic: "To me, it's caring for others and yourself. Genuine care. That means not giving away your soul to make a buck or discounting your value to add a client to your list. The balance is this: you must still sell."

Martin: "I'm not sure I understand the last part of what you said. Discounting your value?"

Nic: "In short Martin, you have value and service. It's worth something. If you sell it for too low a price, you'll know deep down that you are wasting time and energy. Care is fair, on both sides of the fence. For the buyer and the seller. People want to be served without the feeling of being sold. If you are selling with purpose, your customers will feel it."

"Sell with purpose."

Martin: "OK. I think I get it. Can you give me another example though?"

Nic: "Sure. Look at Oprah."

Martin: "Oprah? What does she have to do with Boutique Thinking?"

Nic: "She's a master at it! She takes 'care' to the highest level. She loves in such a big way that everyone loves her back. Advertising on her show is some of the highest priced on television and for many companies is worth every penny and more."

Martin: "I never thought of it that way."

Nic: "So you can see that Boutique Thinking is not just for small start up businesses. The point is: As your business grows, keep an eye on what you care about. If you don't, you can get lost."

Martin: "Do you know of any companies that got lost?"

Nic: "Sure. Take a look right here. These guys have been growing fast right?"

Martin: "Yeah. Seems they are on every street corner."

Nic: "Well, recently, they realized that for the sake of "production" and speed, they would use automatic espresso machines and pre-seal the ground coffee for re-sale."

Martin: "So?"

Nic: "So what ends up happening is the aroma of fresh ground beans is gone when you walk in. The Barista no longer pulls the espresso shots by hand. Gone is the intimate experience, the theatre, the romance!"

Martin: "Whoa! You really do love your coffee."

Nic: "I do! And so do many others who line up to pay more for their coffee. They have realized their mistake and are going back to the core values of what grew this company in the first place."

Martin: "That was a great example. Thanks."

Nic: "My kids also lost their way."

Martin: "Your kids started a business?"

Nic: "Yeah. They started a lemonade stand and kept drinking their own product. Then realized they needed to make up for lost inventory and reduced the amount of lemon juice in the water."

Martin, now laughing: "So what happened?"

Nic: "They didn't get any repeat business. We talked about it over dinner one night and decided to start from scratch."
Martin: "You helped them out?"

Nic: "Just gave a little advice."

Martin: "Nice. What did they do?"

Nic: "They made a new sign. Offered a free sample of their new an improved lemonade and offered extra ice for those who wanted some. They also sang to attract business."

Martin: "How'd they do?"

Nic: "They made enough to pay for their supplies, pay for the ride tickets at the summer exhibition and put 10% into their investing account, which was my fee for the advice I gave them."

Martin: "Nice!"

Nic: "On a larger scale: The Dotcom era. It's not that long ago that many Internet companies were created to "cash in" on the Internet. They came in fast and crashed hard."

Martin: "Good point. I'm guessing they didn't have the systems in place to handle the business."

Nic: "Exactly, or they didn't care."

Martin finished his coffee. Reached his hand out to say good-bye to Nic when a book was thrust into his hand, Big-Box Swindle by Stacy Mitchell."

Martin laughing: "I guess I should have expected that."

Nic: "Yup!"

"Keep an eye on what you care about."

Use Emotions and Get Inspired

The next meeting started once again at 8:00AM for Martin and Nic, coffees in hand.

Nic began with a quote: "Convenience creates demand through inspiration."

Martin nodded and listened.

Nic: "I've come to realize that the people we work with and the customers we care about are always looking for continued inspiration. They just may not be conscious of it."

Martin: "What do you mean?"

Nic: "In the case of people we work with, they need to be more than motivated. Sometimes that is through healthy competition or incentives or simply a pat on the back."

"People we work with require more than motivation, they need inspiration."

Martin: "I understand that. It just seems there's a difference between motivation and inspiration."

Nic: "There is! For our customers, we want them to feed off of our energy and we want them to come back for more. The fact is when those customers come in for a dose of Martin, they are charged up just to see you! The result? You get just as much a charge out of them! How's that for win-win?"

Martin: "Yeah I do love that. I have many "regulars" who pop in and we either smile at each other or high five and some even give me great big hugs. It's awesome!"

The Boutique Agreement

A couple of lattés with extra foam and both Nic and Martin were all smiles.

Nic: "I had one of my mentors recommend a book early in my career and I'm going to recommend the same book to you."

Martin: "You got me now, I'm curious. What's it about?"

Nic: "It's not a big book. It's a "packed" book. It's filled with great ideas and what I call signposts."

Martin: "Signposts?"

Nic: "Yes. A signpost is something that helps me stay on track. So before you leave today, go pick up Think and Grow Rich by Napoleon Hill."

"Signposts are reminders of our goals."

Nic: "To me, what you are holding is one of those books that I prefer not to lend to someone because I want it around as a reminder of all the ideas and signposts it has to offer."

Martin: "Really? Wow. It's must be a good book."

Nic: "It is to me. I give many of the books I read to friends and colleagues. This is one I like to keep in my personal library."

Martin: "You must have quite the library."

Nic: "Well, it's not as vast as this bookstore and I don't have a coffee shop connected to it."

Martin: "Something tells me you can probably make a pretty mean latté."

Nic just smiled.

Nic: "I got inspired with an idea when reading this book. I like to call it the Boutique Agreement."

Martin was listening attentively urging his mentor on with his stare.

Nic: "The exercise is so simple that for some reason, many people don't bother. In fact, I didn't apply Boutique Thinking until it hit me that I'd better or I'd lose it all."

Martin: "You? It's more like you have it all! What's the deal?"

Nic: "Here it is. Write down your goals, set a goal line or what some might call a time frame. Read them with a peer, colleague or someone you admire and respect."

Martin: "OK."

Nic: "Then you sign it and get them to sign as a witness to your commitment."

Martin: "Wow. I'd be scared to do that."

Nic: "If you believe you will fail, you will. If you believe you will succeed, you will. Success is up to you."

Martin took a few moments and a long pull of coffee.

Nic: "The Boutique Agreement is now transformed. It is now a 'living' signpost of your desired outcome. In fact some of my top managers have applied this to become part owners in the restaurants they work in."

Martin: "Out of one agreement?"

Nic: "Yup! Here's the thing. You have to keep reviewing your agreement. Remember, you've made this contract with yourself to reach these goals. And you've also anchored it with the help of a witness. Look it over everyday. At breakfast, for example. I have mine copied on my cell phone, that way I can review it often and with ease."

Martin: "Now that is smart. You must have your phone with you all the time!"

Nic: "It feels like an extra appendage sometimes!"

Martin laughing: "Nice!"

Nic continued: "What I love about making these agreements is I'm reaching them and making new ones. You'll see that you'll be able to set goals, reach them and set new ones and reach them! Life can be as big as I want it to be. Boutique Thinking provides me the CARE I need to invoke the desire and make it real.

"Dream it, Desire it and Make it Real!"

The Boutique Agreement

Write out a goal that you intend to reach. Share it with a friend, family or mentor and commit to reaching your goal by signing your agreement.

I, _____, agree to:

_____
_____
_____
_____
_____
_____
_____
_____
_____
_____
_____
_____
_____
_____
_____
_____
_____

Target Date: _____

X_____   X_____
  Signed   Witness

The Boutique Incentive

Nic and Martin arrived in the parking lot at the same time and headed for the hub of caffeinated people in the bookstore. After securing their table with a frothy latte in hand, they got down to business.

Martin: "I'm having some trouble motivating a couple of my team members."

Nic: "What seems to be the problem?"

Martin: "Well, the other people at the store are all into the commission program I have in place. The thing is, I have two guys who I know can really do a great job. They're just not behind the current system."

Nic: "So what you are doing at the moment is offering money as an incentive."

Martin: "Yeah. Who wouldn't want to have more money?"

Nic: "Not so fast my friend. You'd be surprised how many times I've heard about this kind of thing."

Martin: "Really?"

Nic taking a sip of his coffee: "Mm-hmm. In fact, I've learned that variety in short term incentives is a key factor to motivate staff that may not be with you for the long haul."

Martin: "Short Term Incentives. What do you mean?"

Nic: "Well, money can be motivating for many, that's for sure. Have you ever put on a friendly contest?"

Martin: "For prizes or for free lunches?"

Nic: "Sure."

Martin: "Yeah, they've had that before and it goes over OK I guess."

Nic: "How about a Team Incentive?"

Martin: "What do you mean?"

Nic: "In a Boutique environment, I find it important to remind the team that it's not how many sales we make, it's how many smiles we give and get."

Martin: "Nic, that's corny man."

Nic laughed: "OK. Maybe it is. Yet consider this: If you went back to your Mantra and the rest of your team reflected the same way, would it not make sense? How have you built your business, your specific "Brand Martin", one sale at a time or one relationship at a time?"

Martin: "I'm not concerned with my work ethic. I just want to make sure that my team is motivated."

Nic: "So are you prepared to get to a point to let go?"

Martin, now on the defensive: "What does that mean?"

Nic: "Hey my friend, as a Mentor I'm going to push your buttons sometimes OK?"
Martin sighing: "OK."

Nic: "What I mean by 'Let go' is exactly what Mr. Hobbs is doing with you. Can you let go so your team can have room to breathe, to make mistakes to grow?"

"Let go, so your team can have room to breathe, to make mistakes and grow."

Martin: "I guess that's my challenge."

Nic: "It can be a huge one at that. And once you can truly overcome it, you'll probably find yourself in a place where you wondered what took you so long."

Martin, feeling relieved: "Sounds like you're speaking from experience."

Nic, smiling: "You better believe it. Once I 'let go', many of my 'would-be stars' became superstars because I gave them the room to grow they needed. That also includes the opportunity to make mistakes, be accountable and move on."

Martin: "So I don't have to necessarily offer money all the time?"

Nic: "Nope. You do have a responsibility though."

Martin: "Meaning?"

Nic: "Once a team member is doing awesome 'solo', reward them for allowing you the freedom to do more of what you need to."

Martin: "Nice. That makes sense."

Nic: "So the incentive here is career based. For you it's getting a percentage of Mr. Hobbs business right?"

Martin: "Is it that obvious?"

Nic smiling again: "Just a guess."

Nic tool another sip of his coffee: "Some want profit share, some want management experience, some want extra time off and Mr. Hobbs wants an exit."

Martin took the time to reflect on that for the rest of the day.

Be In The Now

It was 8:00AM on a Saturday morning and Martin was seated with Nic, each with their respective cup of coffee.

Martin: "I've had a tough time with the latest book you gave me. It's very technical."

Nic: "Are you learning anything from it?"

Martin: "I am. That I need at least one of these before reading it." Martin points to his coffee.

Nic smiling: "Good one. OK, I'll know for next time what direction to point you in."

Martin: "Hey! Don't worry about me. I'll read what you give me."

Nic: "I know you will, there is no doubt in that. There's a Boutique Thinking lesson here."

Martin: "I obviously missed something."

Nic: "No you didn't and neither did I."

Martin: "Huh? What do you mean by that?"

Nic: "I mean that a Boutique Thinker is always listening. Based on your reaction to the last book, it seems that you are geared towards certain writing styles. That's good to know."

Martin: "You don't miss a beat do you?"

Nic: "I do my best not to."

Martin: "I'm learning that it's the Boutique way."

Nic with pride: "You're getting it kid!"

"A Boutique Thinker is always listening."

They each took a few sips before Nic spoke up.

Nic: "What are the big plans for today?"

Martin: "Well, like you we have certain days that are busier than others and Saturday's tend to be a big traffic day."

Nic looking at his watch: "I'm not holding you up am I?"

Martin: "Not at all. I'm heading in to the store for 9:00AM this morning with coffee for the staff."

Nic: "That's sporting of you. They must really like that."

Martin: "They do. I like the staff to be in 30 minutes before we open to go over what's in inventory and any issues that may need to be discussed."

Nic: "What kind of issues come up?"

Martin: "Funny you ask because I was going to ask you your advice on a certain situation I'm dealing with."

Nic: "Go ahead."

Martin: "I have a staff member who is producing but isn't putting in more hours."
Nic: "Can you be more specific?"

Martin: "Sure. This guy Kevin is a great salesperson. Out of all the team, he's always in the top 3. The problem is he only works part time."

Nic: "So what's the problem?"

Martin: "He won't take more hours! I'm offering more time to him and he doesn't commit. He just wants part time."

Nic: "Hmm. When he is at work, does he work hard?"

Martin: "Very. I wish all my staff were like him."

Nic: "Got it."

Martin: "Got it? Like you have a solution?"

Nic: "Yup. Let him keep his part time shifts and give him a raise."

Martin in shock: "What?"

Nic: "Well, based on what you are telling me, this Kevin person is you best staff member on an hourly basis. Sounds to me that Kevin is always in the Now."

Martin: "In the Now?"

Nic: "Time for another Boutique Thinking lesson my friend, as well as a recommendation for a book."

Martin: "Lay it on me."

Nic: "The Power of Now by Eckhart Tolle. Being in the Now is being totally immersed in the task at hand. My sense is Kevin is so focused on the moment that he doesn't even worry about the work he needs to do. He just enjoys it all."

Martin: "Have you been spying on the store or something? That's totally what he's like."

Nic: "Don't you ever have those moments Martin? Like time doesn't matter? That is an example of being in the Now."

Martin: "Sure I do. But I'm not always at work when they happen."

Nic laughing: "I sure hope not!"

Martin laughed with his mentor for a moment.

Nic: "The next thing you may want to consider is asking Kevin some questions on his success at work. How does he keep his focus?"

Martin, with hesitation: "Really?"

Nic: "Boutique Thinking again Martin. What is that, three lessons today? After this you're going to have to go, otherwise all of this wisdom will flow out your ears."

Martin: "I can just picture it. OK, I hesitated."

Nic: "Yes you did. This is a lesson not everyone picks up. A real Boutique Thinker has to do this. Ready to hear it?"

Martin: "Ready."

Nic: "Drop the ego."

Martin was speechless.

Nic: "I know its tough to hear this my friend. I tell you because I care. You have to lower your defenses and realize that you can learn at all angles, especially from your own staff. When you apply this, your very own team becomes your greatest ally."

Martin: "I never thought of it that way … I just don't want anyone to lose faith in me."

Nic: "They won't. Those that hear you asking questions will respect you even more."

Martin: "Really?"

Nic: "Absolutely! By asking them questions on how they reach their success, you are letting these individuals know that you value them."

Martin: "I guess I would be."

Nic: "For sure! The systems we have at NR's weren't all from me. They've evolved since my first restaurant, way back when; thanks to all the feedback I got from my very own staff, suppliers and customers."

"Drop your ego and your team becomes your greatest ally."

Nic: "A business that will thrive in the future must align itself with suppliers that are committed to their success and they must have staff they value having. Suppliers exist that cater exclusively to the Boutique Thinkers. Some industries have buying groups and co-operatives. But purchasing is only one part of the battle."

Martin: "That I can understand. Marketing, location, inventory control are important too."

Nic burst in: "People! Boutique Thinking demands investing in yourself and your people. It is _there_, where you can pool the creative energies of your team. Inspiration is a byproduct of *good* training."

"Inspiration is a byproduct of *good* training."

Nic continued: "It is in the best interest of the Boutique Thinker to invest in their people through consistent training and perks. This will ensure long-term commitment and loyalty."

Martin: "How often should I be putting some training together for my team?"

Nic: "ALWAYS my friend. Here is the bottom line: If you don't keep improving yourself and your people, someone else will be expanding into your space. You know I'm a fitness nut."

Martin: "I sure do."

Nic: "Then let me put it this way. You are either getting stronger or you are getting weaker."

Nic let this set in for Martin's sake. They both sat and sipped their coffees for a moment.

Nic continued: "There's this universal law. Where there is a void, someway, somehow, it will be filled."

Martin listened intensely.

Nic: "So, if the law states that if there is a void it's going to get filled: MAKE SURE YOU"RE THE ONE TO FILL IT!"

Martin: "Fill the void. Become the solution!"

Nic: "Exactly! It needs to be understood that money is a byproduct of Boutique Thinking. If we solely focused on money, we may lose our way. It's like a small shop taking on Big Box at the price game."

Martin: "That's not the way, I've learned that the hard way."

Nic: "The balance piece is this: Understanding that the service you provide is the vehicle that warrants the price."

"The service you provide is the vehicle that warrants the price."

Boutique Thinking Strategies

Another brisk morning for Martin, who had a tougher time to get out of bed, as it seemed a little cold. The inspiration hit him when he knew that Nic was getting a coffee order this morning. Martin still arrived early for the meeting.

Nic: "An interesting trend that occurs in many failed specialty businesses is the focus on price."

Martin: "I've been down this road."

Nic: "This misguided focus comes along because of the lack of the right relationship and 'care' questions to clients. The only reason the care piece is missing is the missing 'mantra' link is missing. When these steps are properly followed, the cash register will ring as the Boutique Thinkers take customer care to new levels."

Martin: "I've always felt that my market wants a deal of some kind. To really show the customer we are different."

Nic: "It just doesn't make sense to take a specialized product and discount it purely based on a similar item at a lower price. Even a product that is similar to what is found in a big box can have one or two unique properties that justify the cost. When combined with real care and a solid system, price rarely becomes the issue."

"With real Care, price rarely becomes the issue."

Martin: "I'm not so sure. I keep getting the sense that my customers "demand" a deal or they won't buy."
Nic: "I think it's customers who are tough negotiators. You have the right to be tough in that respect. The fact is people have more access to money than ever before and are not afraid to spend it."

Martin: "Well it's tough to not move on price when Big Box is discounting left right and centre."

Nic: "Ah. The evil price drop rears its ugly head, and the independent retailer tries to compete on price. The sad part of this is even the consumer eventually loses because the quality of the goods they end up having access to can be very limited as too many people got caught up in the 'price war'. What's worse is the specialty store loses valuable profits because they are playing the Big Box game with their rules."

Martin: "So what does a store like the one I'm in do?"

Nic: "It's time to re-evaluate your direction and elevate your game. You don't even want to be playing on the same field as the Big Box. In fact, you don't even want to be playing the same game."

Martin: "So what should my strategy be?"

Nic: "Well, you may want to consider studying your competition. Now in years past that would be other specialty stores in the same field as you."

Martin: "That should be easy enough."

Nic: "Hang on there's more."

Martin, with a little fun in his voice: "I'm not surprised."

Nic, with the same fun right back at his pupil: "Hey, buddy. You want the goods or what?"
Martin: "Please!"

Nic, laughing now: "OK. As years go by for any business, they start to look beyond their niche and look at the big box guys. The Costco, Sears and Wal-Marts of the world for example."

Martin: "The enemy."

Nic: "I'd suggest you don't look at them like that."

Martin: "They're not the bad guys?"

Nic: "Nope, they're just different. And they do what they do very well."

Martin, hesitating: "OK."

Nic: "We have to understand that these Big Box guys are tough to deal with for suppliers. They grind them down to as little profit as possible. Generally speaking, the products found in the Big Box stores are dated in comparison to what you'll find in the specialists."

Martin: "But how does this apply to you Mr. NR Restaurants?"

Nic after a long pull of his coffee: "Here's an interesting tip for you my friend. Many of my specials are not discounted, in fact they are items not regularly found on my or anyone else's menu. For my business, it is my service that makes NR's special."

Martin: "OK."

Nic: "I make significantly higher profits on meal specials than I do on my signature dishes."

Another light bulb went off for Martin: "Oh man. That makes sense!"

Nic: "I don't have thousands of locations where billions are being served."

Martin: "I noticed you didn't have any clowns either."

Nic with a laugh: "No I don't. But I do get some discounts on the raw foods I need for my high selling signature items. The big chains get deeper discounts."

Martin: "OK, but their product or their quality isn't even in the same ballpark as what you offer."

Nic paused and smiled: "You understand Grasshopper."

Nic: "Your biggest competitor is YOU. If you want to get caught up in a price war against a juggernaut, the odds are pretty good you're going to lose."

"Your biggest competitor is YOU."

Martin: "So are you saying I should bring in expensive stuff?"

Nic: "I never said that. I would suggest you do your due diligence to offer your clients the products and services that coincide with your Mantra and the code of customer care. In most cases you'll end up with the differences you need to out-smart and outmaneuver the Big Box."

Martin: "I like that."

Nic: "I thought you would. Use the Big Box's size to your advantage. They generally purchase their goods long before you would. Sometimes their buying programs are set up to 12 months in advance."

Martin: "Wow. That must be tough to manage."

Nic: "Maybe, but that really doesn't concern us. What should concern us is knowing that we can have certain products that the Big Box don't and can't access."

The Signpost

For the first time in a long time, Martin met Nic for an afternoon coffee. Martin arrived early so he could have a look around at some of the new arrivals on the bookshelves. It didn't surprise Martin at all to find his mentor in the aisles. What did surprise him was the section.

Martin: "Look who's early. Why am I not surprised?"

Nic: "Just having a quick peek before you got here."

Martin: "The business section is that way. What are you doing in the philosophy section?"

Nic: "If you had been here 3 minutes earlier, you would have seen me perusing through the spirituality section."

Martin paused: "Are you looking for something in particular?"

Nic: "Not in particular. I am always looking to grow my thinking and mindset. Sometimes at the back of a book that I really enjoyed, there's a recommended reading list."

Martin: "Sure, I've seen them in some of the books you picked for me."

Nic: "Well for me, those selections are just signposts for me to be aware of."

Martin: "Signposts?"

Nic: "Let's grab a coffee and sit down for this one."
The two strolled to the counter and ordered lattes and sat in a couple of cozy leather chairs.

Martin: "So what's the scoop with the signposts?"

Nic took a sip of hot coffee: "Signposts are reminders of the direction you want to be going in."

Martin: "Makes sense."

Nic: "I look for signposts in the various books I read to make sure I'm headed in the right direction both personally and professionally. In this case, I'm looking at different book titles in non-business sections of the store. Remember the lesson of Out of Office Learning?"

Martin: "Sure."

Nic: "Well, not all of my business ideas come from business books."

Martin: "That's true. I've learned a lot from a novel Jen gave me 2 months ago."

Nic smiled: "Your mantra is not only corporate, it is individual. As a Boutique Thinker, the need to validate your course of action in the caring of customers is very important. If you are leading a team of people in your store or organization, everyone's values must be on the same wavelength or the team won't gel as good as it should."

"As a Boutique Thinker, you must validate your course of action in the caring of your customers."

Martin: "It seems that the team can forget where we're headed."

Nic: "So talk about your direction, often! This doesn't mean Death By Meeting. Notes on a corkboard, broadcast e-mails and voice mails can do this. I like to involve all my team members to be responsible for a message to the rest of us. This way we are all building our corporate culture together as one team. This comes from my dishwashers all the way to my GM's."

Martin: "Even your dishwashers?"

"Involve all your team members."

Nic: "Absolutely! I have 2 managers who have been with me since they were teens. They've learned the business from the ground up and have helped me grow in the process. They've made notes that were humorous and insightful for staff at all levels to understand."

Martin: "My guess is that Big Box doesn't do that."

Nic: "I haven't heard of it. The beauty of Boutique Thinking is regardless of how big my company gets, I'm going to keep my 'family' together."

Martin: "Sweet!"

Nic: "Yup!"

Boutique Quotes

Write down messages that are reminders of what you and your team are doing. Quotes can come from staff members, a line from a song, a movie or a famous speech. Have fun with this one. Broadcast them to your team. Place them on Post It notes and invite your team to do the same. You'll be surprised with the results!

_____

_____

_____

_____

_____

_____

_____

_____

_____

_____

_____

Boutique Thinking Online

Martin arrived for his latest morning meeting with Nic working away on his laptop on a corner table. Martin waved at Nic and pointed to the menu board. He was 'mouthing' to Nic if he wanted a coffee? Nic simply raised his cup and shook his head and lipped "Thanks anyways".

Martin sat down and Nic packed his laptop away.

Martin: "Checking up on your stocks?"

Nic: "Actually, I was checking in on the latest NR's web site."

Martin: "Selling stuff there?"

Nic: "Only the NR's concept my friend, to those who choose to visit the site."

Martin: "What about the Internet? Technically a business can become a juggernaut online."

Nic: "If it were that easy, I'd have done it already."

Martin, speaking into his coffee cup: "Knowing you, I have to agree."

Nic: "The Internet is a medium my friend. And it can certainly help your purpose as a Boutique Thinker."

Martin: "What do you mean?"

Nic: "I find the Internet is an additional tool to promote and get feedback from my client base. I know you have used the Internet to do your sales promotions as well."

Martin smiled and listened.

Nic: "For the Boutique Thinker, the Internet is a legitimacy stamp."

Martin: "What do you mean?"

Nic: "It's a fact of life my friend. If you don't have a website, you are behind in the times. And now you can't just have a website, you need to have something captivating for your specific target."

Martin: "OK."

Nic: "Take these guys for example. Do you think they sell many lattés on-line?"

Martin: "I wouldn't think so. And the delivery would be an issue."

Nic, laughing: "Exactly. If you've ever taken your laptop in with you for a coffee, you are immediately taken to their home page first."

Martin: "And I notice there are more laptops and handheld devices tuning in all the time."

Nic smiling: "Ah, very perceptive grasshopper. All the more reason to have your legitimacy stamp online."

"The Internet is a legitimacy stamp."

Martin, sounding a little overwhelmed: "I don't have the time to build a web-site."

Nic: "You don't have time not to build a website. You have to pay for someone to do it for you and you have to an active roll in its progress."

Martin, still overwhelmed: "Where do I start?"

Nic: "Martin, don't stress on this. One of the biggest problems for Boutique Thinkers is they think they have to have a site as good as Apple. Start off with the basics and go from there."

Martin: "I guess I'm going to be in touch with a web page service."

Nic: "If you have a single page and it looks good and provides the basics, it is significantly better than having 100 pages and there is no point to it. Again, THINK BOUTIQUE when putting your site together. Nothing hugely elaborate and certainly not confusing."

Martin: "Many of my customers would say they are *computarted*."

Nic, laughing: "Is that a technical term?"

Martin, smiling: "Yeah."

Nic: "Well if that is the way they feel about computers and technology, all the more reason for your site to be easy. Here's a secret in Boutique Thinking: Simplicity is Elegant."

"Simplicity is Elegant."

Martin: "I like that."

Nic: "So will your customers my friend. Boutique Thinking is about convenience, service and passion."

Martin: "So what is simply elegant on-line?"

Nic: "Look at Google for example. They weren't the first in the game when it came to search engines. They did understand who their clients were. It wasn't kids; it was adults who wanted a simple way to search for something. Google nailed it and continued listening to what their clients wanted."

Martin: "But Nic, Google is far from being a Boutique."

Nic: "I understand that, and so do they! They're huge! And they think like a Boutique. Martin, Boutique Thinking doesn't mean small thinking. It means *passion* thinking, focused on my goal thinking. Boutique Thinking is care based thinking which turns into big results."

Words of the Boutique

It had been a year since Martin met Nicholas Robinson. In that time, Martin read 16 books, attended 4 seminars and was receiving positive inspiration daily via his e-mail.

Once again it was Martin who headed into the bookstore with the intention to meet his mentor.

The steam coming from the mug of coffee in the early morning air was hypnotic. Either that or Martin needed the caffeine to kick in.

Nic: "How you feeling?"
Martin: "Flipping' cold this morning."
Nic took in a deep breath: "Ah! That morning air is refreshing though. I figured taking a stroll with our coffees could inspire some different kind of energy for us."

Martin, sipping: "Mmm. This does taste good out here."

Nic: "You've brought to light an interesting thought."

Martin: "What did I do?"

Nic: "You used the word 'flipping' to describe the cold."

Martin looking inquisitive: "You've never heard that before?"

Nic: "Sure. It got your point across very well. That's the power of words."

Martin: "Ah, the next lesson?"

Nic: "Yup!"

Martin: "I'm all ears."

Nic: "In any organization, be it a retail store, big box or not, we have one thing in common."

Martin: "What's that?"

Nic: "We are all marketing."

"We are all marketing."

Nic took a sip and Martin was anxious to hear what came next.

Nic: "One of the major differences in the kind of "service" a Boutique Thinker provides to their clients is in the use of their words in relation to the solutions they provide."

Martin: "I'm not sure I follow."

Nic: "Let me give you one tiny example from NR's."

Martin: "Shoot."

Nic: "Imagine you and Jen are eating a meal at a restaurant."

Martin: "That's easy."

Nic smiled: "Now, you are both having a bite of your meal and of course it is at that moment your server comes by and asks you: How is everything?"

Martin: "OK."

Nic: "Next time you have dinner at NR's please note that your server will ask you a different question."

The light bulb flashed to the ON position for Martin: "You're right. In fact the last time we ate there, our server came by and asked us something else."

Nic jumped in: "Exactly. They may have asked: "How are the flavors?" "Isn't that a great combination?"

Martin: "Yeah, something like that. Jen always says that it's cool the way your team takes care of us."

Nic: "That's the power of words my friend. It's not that the other restaurants or businesses don't have the 'ask' piece in the systems. It is how we are *implementing* them that separates us."

"How you implement your words makes a difference."

Martin: "But can something that seems so trivial really make that much of a difference?"

Nic: "Absolutely. Every piece amplifies. Next time you're at NR's listen to the marketing the server will provide on the specials. They are promoting."

Martin: "I know! It's like a Broadway play!"

Nic: "Alright smart guy. I wouldn't go that far."

Martin: "Your staff is incredibly energized when they talk specials. They really crank it up."
Nic: "Remember what we talked about when we first met? Reflect. You take your energy and think about it, you embody it and what happens is you end up sending it out to those around you."

Martin: "Remember it? I'm living it!"

Nic: "Have you noticed a change in your staff since you have taken the time to reflect?"

Martin: "Yeah."

Nic: "Have you noticed a change in your customers since you've taken the time to reflect?"

Martin: "Big Time!"

Nic: "No doubt. The Boutique Thinker reflects and the staff and customers amplify what you are doing."

"Reflect and Amplify."

Martin: "So the key is stay focused, keep reflecting."

Nic: "And you'll affect people's lives. Big Box generally doesn't think this way. So reflect."

Martin smiled as the message truly sunk in. He was living proof.

Nic smiled back: "Boutique Thinking my friend."

The both smiled at each other over the rims of their coffee cups.

Living The Dream

Martin walked in to the bookstore with a smile that beamed. He was early for his meeting with Nic and ordered a couple of lattés. Nic walked in shortly after Martin had sat down.

Nic: "Nice and early with coffee on the table? Well done!"

Martin: "Thank you. And *Thank You* Nic."

Nic: "Thank me? You bought the coffee my young friend. I should be doing the thanking."

Martin: "OK. You're welcome."

Martin was beaming and Nic could tell he was bursting at the seams.

Nic: "OK. Let's have it."

Martin very sarcastically: "Have what?"

Nic laughing: "Yeah right. Come on! Did you get your deal with Mr. Hobbs?"

Martin: "YES! You are looking at a shareholder to the next location of Hobbs' Inc."

Nic laughing: "Congratulations! You've done it!"

Martin: "Thank you so much Nic. I couldn't have done it without you!"

Nic: "I've learned so much too my friend. I love this energy right now. Enjoy the moment!"

Martin paused: "What happens now?"

Nic: "What do you mean?"

Martin: "I feel I have so much more to learn."

Nic: "We do my friend. Boutique Thinking demands we be continually learning and giving. I'll be on your team for as long as you like."

Martin: "You've just lowered my stress level by like half."

Nic laughing: "Wow. I wish I could have that affect on everyone!"

Martin smiled then started laughing when Nic miraculously manifested a book and handed it to Martin.

Martin: "How do you do that?"

They both laughed.

Epilogue

It was Sunday evening, when most people are home with their families; a couple of entrepreneurial spirits were working hard putting some of the final touches on a new Hobbs location.

Lori, one of the staff who worked with Martin in the store asked him a question during the renovations of the soon to be 2nd location.

Lori: "So you now 'own' a percentage of this location?"

Martin happily answered: "Yup!"

Lori: "You are one lucky guy. How'd you score it Martin?"

Martin: "You want to know? Really?"

Lori very enthusiastic: "Yeah!"

Martin: "You drink coffee in the morning?"

Conclusion

Boutique Thinking requires some effort. Implementing any change in a business is a lot harder than it looks. It takes a lot of practice and persistence. Nothing worth achieving comes easy.

Just as a fitness program requires consistency in exercise, so it is with improving your business and your sales.

Like Martin, I urge you to find a mentor or a coach that you can learn and gain valuable insights from. It is also important to continue the education process and surround yourself by the conditions you truly want to produce. This is why I also strongly encourage you to become a mentor for either your staff, family or member of your community. It is very rewarding and lends itself for opportunities to learn more about your business and yourself. Remember that mentors can be any age. I've learned so much from my kids.

The biggest competitors we have are ourselves. Place your focus on opportunities, not obstacles. Stay in contact with your customers and be consistent with your ability to offer them value, results and thanks.

Serve All and Be Awesome!

Suggested Reading

George, Bill, *Authentic Leadership* Jossey-Bass, 2003.

Gladwell, Malcolm, *The Tipping Point,* Little Brown and Company, 2005.

Smith, B. & Rutigliano, T. *Discover Your Sales Strengths,* Warner, 2003.

Tolle, Eckhart, *The Power of Now,* Namaste 1999.

Kiyosaki, Robert, *Rich Dad Poor Dad,* Warner,1998.

Waters, Robyn, *The Trendmaster's Guide,* Penguin Group, 2005.

Godin, Seth, *Purple Cow,* Penguin Group, 2002.

Blanchard, Ken & Bowles, Sheldon, *Raving Fans,* William Morrow and Company, 1993.

Connellan, Thomas, *Brining Out the Best in Others,* Bard Press, 2003.

Johnson, Spencer, *Who Moved My Cheese?,* G.P. Putnam's Sons, 1998.

Peters, Tom, *Re-imagine!,* DK, 2003.

Be a Boutique Thinker
And join the B.T.T.
(It's Free!)

Want to be a part of the Boutique Thinking Team? (BTT)
Have an inspirational story to tell?
Are you or someone you know doing something in their small business to thrive against the Big Box?

Join for FREE at www.boutiquethinking.com/BTT

There are plenty of small business owners, sales people and entrepreneurs of all ages who are looking for that one ingredient that will propel them to the next level. The BTT is a forum for various small business leaders, owners, managers and staff members to share their thoughts and systems to be able to compete and thrive against the Big Box stores.

As Boutique Thinkers, we are swift, light on our feet and make faster decisions that we can implement at lightening speeds. Together, we can lift each other up to highly competitive levels.

Join right now and share some inspiration!

Joe Marcoux and his company, Just Did IT Inc, are available for sales training and workshops.

Visit www.justdidit.biz for more information.

To Contact Joe Marcoux:
joe@justdidit.biz

Just Did IT
257 Thomas Berry St.
Winnipeg, MB
R2H 0R2
(204) 233-6048

978-0-595-44527-1
0-595-44527-6

Printed in the United States
84714LV00003B/139-186/A